Special Education

A Practical Approach to Educating Disables

Nirmala Thapar

Saurabh
Publishing House
4735/22, Prakash Deep Building,
Ansari Road, Daryaganj,
New Delhi- 110002

Published by :
SAURABH PUBLISHING HOUSE

Distributed by :
Lotus Press Publishers & Distributors
Unit No. 220, 2nd Floor, 4735/22, Prakash Deep Building,
Ansari Road, Darya Ganj, New Delhi- 110002
Ph.: 41325510, 09811838000
• E-mail : lotuspress1984@gmail.com
www.lotuspress.co.in

Saurabh Publishing House is an imprint of
Lotus Press Publishers & Distributors

Special Education : A Practical Approach to Educating Disables

ISBN: 978-81-89005-01-6 (HB)

Printed by : **Lotus Press Publishers & Distributors, New Delhi**

CONTENTS

1

SPECIAL EDUCATION: CURRICULUM

Education is a powerful instrument of social change, and often initiates upward movement in the social structure. Thereby, helping to bridge the gap between the different sections of society. The educational scene in India has undergone major change over the years, resulting in better provision of education and better educational practices. In 1944, the Central Advisory Board of Education (CABE) published a comprehensive report called the Sergeant Report on the post-war educational development of the country. As per the report, provisions for the education of the handicapped, were to form an essential part of the national system of education, which was to be administered by the Education Department. According to this report, handicapped children were to be sent to special schools only when the nature and extent of their defects made this necessary.

The Kothari Commission (1964–66), the first Education Commission of independent India, observed: "the education of the handicapped children should be an inseparable part of the education system." The Commission recommended experimentation with integrated programmes in order to bring as many children as possible into these programmes.

The government's agenda to universalize elementary education, and its commitment to the Directive Principles of the Constitution, are guided by the recognition that a new universal system of education should be based on equity, the redressal of past imbalances, and the provision of access to quality education, especially for marginalized groups. Recent educational developments and the Seventy Third and Seventy Fourth Constitutional Amendments outline the possibility of entrusting basic education to the local elected bodies in towns and villages. This would allow for community participation in education at the elementary level and would introduce radical change, leading to the empowerment of learners with Special Educational Needs (SEN).

Until the 1970s, the policy encouraged segregation. Most educators believed that children with physical, sensory, or intellectual disabilities were so different that they could not participate in the activities of a common school. Christian missionaries, in the 1880s, started schools for the disabled as charitable undertakings. The first school for the blind was established in 1887. An institute for the deaf and mute, was set up in 1888. Services for the physically disabled were also initiated in the middle of the twentieth century. Individuals with mental retardation were the last to receive attention. The first school for the mentally challenged being established in 1934. Special education programmes in earlier times were, therefore, heavily dependent on voluntary initiative.

The Government's (Department of Education) initiatives after independence were manifested in the establishment of a few workshop units meant primarily for blind adults. These units later included people who were deaf, physically impaired, and mentally retarded. While some provisions existed in the States, it was considered the best course to assist and encourage voluntary organizations already working in the field. The welfare approach continued in government programmes. Support was provided to voluntary organizations for the establishment of model schools for the blind, the deaf, and the mentally retarded. The government set up the National Library for the Blind, the Central Braille Press, and employment exchanges for the disabled. It also made provisions for scholarships, for prevention and early identification of disabling conditions, for the development of functional skills, and for aids and appliances for the disabled.

LEARNERS WITH SPECIAL EDUCATIONAL NEEDS (SEN)

In India, a learner with SEN is defined variously in different documents. For example, a child with SEN in a District Primary Education Programme (DPEP) document is defined as a child with disability, namely, visual, hearing, locomotor, and intellectual. However, the country report in the NCERT-UNESCO regional workshop report titled *Assessment of Needs for Inclusive Education*: Report of the First Regional Workshop for SAARC countries states that SEN goes beyond physical disability. It also refers to, ...

> the large proportion of children—in the school age—belonging to the groups of child labour are, street children, victims of natural catastrophes and social conflicts, and those in extreme social and economic deprivation. These children constitute the bulk of dropouts from the school system. The SSA Framework for Implementation covers children with Special Needs (SN) under the section on Special Focus Groups. While separating children with disabilities from other groups like girls, Scheduled Castes (SC), Scheduled Tribes (ST), and urban deprived children, it makes provisions for these children under the section on SEN. The Department of Education of Groups with SN in the NCERT itself, initiates programmes for meeting the

learning needs of the disabled and the socially disadvantaged and marginalized, such as the SCs, STs, and minorities.

According to the International Standard Classification of Education, the term Special Needs Education (SNE) means educational intervention and support designed to address SEN. The term "SNE" has come into use as a replacement for the term "Special Education". The earlier term was mainly understood to refer to the education of children with disabilities that takes place in special schools or institutions distinct from, and outside of, the institutions of the regular school and university system. In many countries today a large proportion of disabled children are in fact educated in institutions under the regular system. Moreover, the concept of children with SEN extends beyond those who may be included in handicapped categories to cover those who are failing in school, for a wide variety of reasons that are known to be likely impediments to a child's optimal progress. Whether or not this more broadly defined group of children is in need of additional support, depends on the extent to which schools need to adapt their curriculum, teaching, and organization and/or to provide additional human or material resources so as to stimulate efficient and effective learning for these pupils.

However, only in a few instances and documents, across the various States of the country, has SEN been accepted in its broad perspective. On the whole, the focus has remained on learners with specific disabilities. This view is supported by the fact that the draft Inclusive Education Scheme, available on the website of the Ministry of Human Resources Development (MHRD), which addresses the needs of learners with disabilities, focuses on the following categories of disability: visual disabilities (blind and low vision), speech and hearing disabilities, locomotor disabilities, and neuromusculoskeltal and neuro-developmental disorders, including cerebral palsy, autism, mental retardation, multiple disability, and learning disabilities.

There is ample evidence that women with disabilities experience major psychosocial problems, including depression, stress, lowered self-esteem, and social isolation, which remain largely neglected. Evidence also suggests that women tend to be restricted to home-based activities, while men are likely to be supported in more public and outward-looking avenues. Stereotypes are artefacts of culture that can only be understood by exploring their relations to each other in the cultural system. Gender stereotypes interact with disability stereotypes to constitute a deep matrix of gendered disability in every culture, developed within specific historical contexts, and affecting those contexts over time. While language is the most analyzed site for the examination of both gender and disability, they interact in many other cultural locations—cinema, television, fiction, clothing, and body language. Thus, cultures sustain the social relations of gendered disability in constant reiterations of stereotypes and expectations. In the education scene, discrimination on account of gender has been reported in many studies. However, girls with disabilities have remained invisible both from the writings on gender and on disability. Therefore, the needs of girls with disabilities may be more special than needs of any other group and have to be addressed in all spheres of education.

SHIFTING MODELS OF DISABILITY

The shifting approaches to disability have translated into very diverse policies and practices. The various models of disability impose differing responsibilities on the States, in terms of action to be taken, and they suggest significant changes in the way disability is understood.

Law, policy, programmes, and rights instruments reflect two primary approaches or discourses: disability as an individual pathology and as a social pathology. Within these two overriding paradigms, the four major identifiable formulations of disability are: the charity model, the bio-centric model, the functional model, and the human rights model.

Charity Model

The charity approach gave birth to a model of custodial care, causing extreme isolation and the marginalization of people with disabilities. Unfortunately, in some contemporary practices the reflection of this model can still be traced. For instance, the findings of an investigative project undertaken by the National Human Rights Commission of India between 1997–99 confirmed that a large number of mental health institutions today are still being managed and administered on the custodial model of care—characterized by prison-like structures with high walls, watchtowers, fenced wards, and locked cells. These institutions functioned like detention centres, where persons with mental illness were kept chained, resulting in tragedies like the one at "Erwadi" in Tamil Nadu, in which more than 27 inmates of such a centre lost their lives.

Bio-centric Model

The contemporary bio-centric model of disability regards disability as a medical or genetic condition. The implication remains that disabled persons and their families should strive for "normalization", through medical cures and miracles. Although, biology is no longer the only lens through which disability is viewed in law and policy, it continues to play a prominent role in determining programme eligibility, entitlement to benefits, and it also influences access to rights and full social participation.

A critical analysis of the development of the charity and bio-centric models suggests that they have grown out of the "vested interests" of professionals and the elite to keep the disabled "not educable" or declare them mentally retarded (MR) children and keep them out of the mainstream school system, thus using the special schools as a "safety valve" for mainstream schools. Inclusive education offers an opportunity to restructure the entire school system, with particular reference to the curriculum, pedagogy, assessment, and above all the meaning of education.

Functional Model

In the functional model, entitlement to rights is differentiated according to judgements of individual incapacity and the extent to which a person is perceived as being independent to exercise his/her rights. For example, a child's right to education is dependent on whether or not the child can access the school and participate in the classroom, rather than the obligation being on the school system becoming accessible to children with disabilities.

Human Rights Model

The human rights model positions disability as an important dimension of human culture, and it affirms that all human beings are born with certain inalienable rights. The relevant concepts in this model are:

Diversity

The Greek philosopher, Aristotle, once said that "things that are alike should be treated alike, whereas things that are unalike should be treated unalike in proportion to their un-alikeness." The principle of respect for difference and acceptance of disability as part of human diversity and humanity is important, as disability is a universal feature of the human condition.

Breaking down barriers

Policies that are ideologically based on the human rights model start by identifying barriers that restrict disabled persons' participation in society. This has shifted the focus in the way environments are arranged. In education, for example, where individuals were formerly labelled as not educable, the human rights model examines the accessibility of schools in terms of both physical access and pedagogical strategies.

Equality and non-discrimination

In international human rights law, equality is founded upon two complementary principles: non-discrimination and reasonable differentiation. The doctrine of differentiation is of particular importance to persons with disabilities, some of who may require specialized services or support in order to be placed on a basis of equality with others. Differences of treatment between individuals are not discriminatory if they are based on "reasonable and objective justification". Moreover, equality not only implies preventing discrimination, but goes far beyond, in remedying discrimination. In concrete terms, it means embracing the notion of positive rights, affirmative action, and reasonable accommodation.

Reasonable accommodation

It is important to recognize that reasonable accommodation is a means by which conditions for equal participation can be achieved, and it requires the burden of accommodation to be in proportion to the capacity of the entity. In the draft *Comprehensive and Integral and International Convention on Protection and Promotion of the Rights and Dignity of Persons with Disabilities,* "reasonable accommodation" has been defined as the "introduction of necessary and appropriate measures to enable a person with a disability fully to enjoy fundamental rights and freedoms and to have access without prejudice to all structures, processes, public services, goods, information, and other systems."

Accessibility

The United Nations Economic and Special Commission for Asia and the Pacific (UNESCAP) has defined "accessibility" as "the measure or condition of things and services that can readily be reached or used by people including those with disabilities".

Equal participation and inclusion

By focusing on the inherent dignity of the human being, the human rights model places the individual at centre stage, in all decisions affecting him/her. Thus, the human rights model, respects the autonomy and freedom of choice of the disabled, and also ensures that they, themselves, prioritize the criteria for support programmes.

It requires that people with disabilities, and other individuals and institutions fundamental to society, are enabled to gain the capacity for the free interaction and participation vital to an inclusive society.

Private and public freedoms

The human rights approach to disability on the one hand requires that the States play an active role in enhancing the level of access to public freedoms, and on the other requires that the enjoyment of rights by persons with disabilities is not hampered by third-party actors in the private sphere. Educational institutions and industry, both in the public and private sectors, should ensure equitable treatment to persons with disabilities.

SPECIAL EDUCATION PROVISIONS IN INDIA

Integrated Education

In the 1970s, the government launched the Centrally Sponsored Scheme of Integrated Education for Disabled Children (IEDC). The scheme aimed at providing educational opportunities to learners with disabilities in regular schools, and to facilitate their achievement and retention. The objective was to integrate children with disabilities in the general community at all levels as equal partners to prepare them for normal development and to enable them to face life with courage and confidence. A cardinal feature of the scheme was the liaison between regular and special schools to reinforce the integration process.

Meanwhile, the National Council of Educational Research and Training (NCERT) joined hands with UNICEF and launched Project Integrated Education for Disabled Children (PIED) in the year 1987, to strengthen the integration of learners with disabilities into regular schools. An external evaluation of this project in 1994 showed that not only did the enrolment of learners with disabilities increase considerably, but the retention rate among disabled children was also much higher than the other children in the same blocks. In 1997, IEDC was amalgamated with other major basic education projects like the DPEP and the *Sarva Shiksha Abhiyan* (SSA).

The IEDC scheme provides for a wide range of incentives and interventions for the education of children with disabilities. These include preschool training, counselling for parents, allowances for books and stationery, uniforms, transport, readers and escorts, hostel facilities, and other assistive devices. The scheme provides one special teacher for every eight children with disabilities, community involvement, and a resource room in a cluster of eight to 10 schools. A number of voluntary organizations are implementing the scheme in the various States.

The enactment of legislations by the State Governments has helped in facilitating access to education for all learners with SEN by introducing various entitlements like reservations, scholarships, allowances, etc. By promulgating the equal rights of learners with SEN, these Acts have significantly impacted the educational policies both at the Central and State levels, but the effect has been marginal.

About 11 per cent of disabled persons between the ages of 5-18 years were enrolled in special schools in the urban areas as compared to less than 1 per cent in the rural areas. This clearly indicates that the presence of special schools in a parallel stream does effect the enrollment of children with disabilities in regular schools. Despite the efforts of governmental and Non-Governmental Organizations (NGOs), there is still a significant need to facilitate access of disabled children to educational institutions and to education in general.

The first and foremost strategy for any country, and especially India, must be therefore to increase the access to education for learners with SEN. Though awareness is being created by the inclusion of learners with SEN in major educational programmes like the DPEP and now the SSA, most of them address SEN as a segregated issue rather than as one that runs through all initiatives. This is supported by the fact that under the SSA, training, linkages with parents, salaries of special educators, aids and appliances, etc. are all provided through the separate provision of Rs.1200 per disabled child per annum. The total money available for such services thus depends on the number of disabled children identified. In addition, access to curriculum and physical access to the school are also issues that need to be addressed immediately.

Though the integration of children with SEN has gathered momentum in the country since 1974, there are other possibilities for these children to gain an education. For example, the National Institute of Open Schooling offers courses that have the advantage of being specially adapted to the needs of every child as well as giving the child every opportunity to progress at his/her own pace. Another example is Alternative Schooling and community-based rehabilitation programmes.

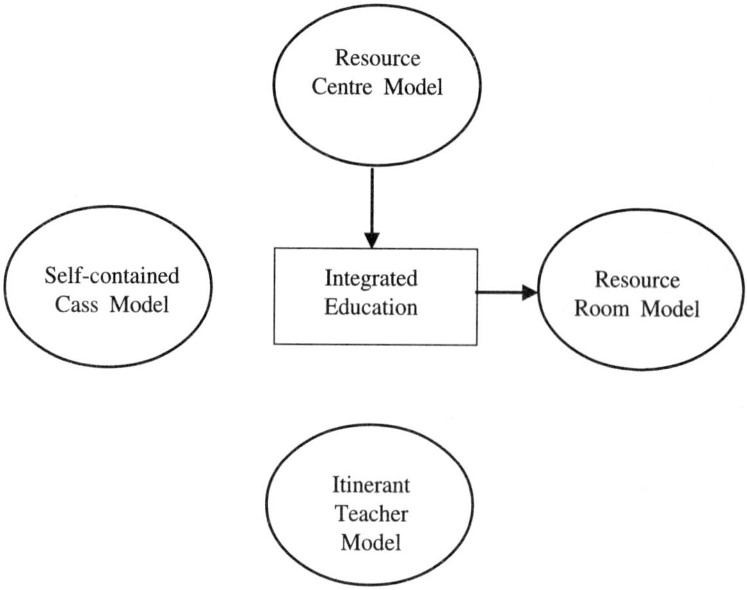

Figure 1: Depicts some of the popular models of Integrated Education being practised in India

It is believed that the fundamental right to education will bring more students with SEN into ordinary schools, which will in turn provide an impetus for change and bring about a number of innovations in the field of SNE.

Legislation

The right of every child to education is proclaimed in the

Universal Declaration of Human Rights and was strongly reaffirmed by the Jometien World Declaration of Education for All. Furthermore, the Standard Rules on the Equalization of Opportunities for Persons with Disabilities was an important resolution to improve the educational conditions of persons with disabilities. This had major implications for the Indian situation in the form of three legislative Acts—The Rehabilitation Council of India Act, 1992 (RCI Act), the Persons with Disabilities (Equal Opportunities, Protection of Rights and Full Participation) Act, 1995 (PWD Act), and the National Trust for Welfare of Persons with Autism, Cerebral Palsy, Mental Retardation and Multiple Disabilities Act, 1999. While the RCI Act was solely concerned with manpower development for the rehabilitation of persons with disabilities, the PWD Act comprises 14 chapters and is a significant endeavour to empower persons with disabilities and promote their equality and participation by eliminating discrimination of all kinds. It emphasizes the need to prepare a comprehensive education scheme that will make various provisions for transport facilities, removal of architectural barriers, supply of books, uniforms, and other materials, the grant of scholarships, suitable modification of the examination system, restructuring of curriculum, providing amanuensis to blind and low vision students, and setting up of appropriate fora for the redressal of grievances. The National Trust Act aims at providing total care to persons with mental retardation and cerebral palsy and also manages the properties bequeathed to the trust.

Changing Role of Special Schools

Special schools have been setup in the past and provisions have been made for integrated education. In 1947, India had a total of 32 such schools for the blind, 30 for the deaf, and three for the mentally retarded. The number of such schools increased to around 3000 by the year 2000. Thus India at present has what Pijl and Meijer refer to as "two tracks". In other words, it has parallel but separate policies on segregation and integration.

Special schools for children with visual impairment, hearing impairment, and locomotor disabilities are streamlined to follow a curriculum that is almost in line with the general education curriculum. The plus curriculum and the adaptation of instructional methodologies are followed where necessary. Children with mental retardation on the other hand require a specialized curriculum to meet their specific educational needs.

Over time, however, there has been growing awareness that special education in special schools may be overly restrictive, and instead of working outside the mainstream classrooms, the special schools can work with, and provide support to, regular schools. Early in 1992, the Programme of Action, while promoting integrated education, had also suggested a Pragmatic Placement Principle. It postulated that learners with disabilities who can be educated in general schools should be educated in general schools, and those studying in special schools should be transferred to general schools once they are ready to make the shift. This was endorsed in 1994 by the Salamanca Statement recommendations for an alternative role for special schools. Hence, special schools in their newfound identity would become a far more flexible resource, by working in partnership with and creating a response to special needs, not only in the alternative form of provision and intervention, but within the mainstream classroom, curricula, and pedagogies. Special and general education, in other words, are gearing for a significant move to come closer together. Briefly stated, the education of persons with disabilities in India has been recognized as an integral part of the educational system, hence, the policies and programmes adopted in recent years have been in accordance with this belief.

Inclusive Education

The National Curriculum Framework for School Education (NCFSE), brought out by the NCERT, recommended inclusive schools for all without specific reference to pupils with SEN as a way of providing quality education to all learners According to NCFSE:

> Segregation or isolation is good neither for learners with disabilities nor for general learners without disabilities. Societal requirement is that learners with special needs should be educated along with other learners in inclusive schools, which are cost effective and have sound pedagogical practices.

The NCFSE also recommended definitive action at the level of curriculum makers, teachers, writers of teaching–learning materials, and evaluation experts for the success of this strategy. This precipitated a revision of the IEDC scheme. This revision is in progress and has, to a certain extent, gained ground in the country.

Internationally, until the end of 1980s, integration remained the main issue whenever discussions were held regarding the rights of disabled persons to an appropriate education. Whereas, in India, integration was a major reform of the 1970s, the need for inclusive education became evident from the fact that despite complete financial support under the IEDC scheme, for integrating learners with special needs into the educational system, only 2–3 per cent of the total population of these learners was actually integrated into the regular schools. Dissatisfaction with the progress towards integration, consideration of costs involved, and the advantages of an inclusive environment in bringing about increased acceptance of learners with SEN, led to demands for more radical change. The constant use of the medical model of assessment, wherein educational difficulties are explained solely in terms of defects in the child, led to a re-conceptualization of the special needs (SN) task as requiring school reforms and improved pedagogy. This re-conceptualization at the both the international and national level helped in the emergence of an orientation towards inclusive education. In the 1990s, inclusion captured the field after the World Conference on Special Needs Education in Salamanca in 1994, with the adoption of the Salamanca Statement and Framework for Action on Special Needs Education. This statement, which was adopted by the representatives of 92 governments and 25 international organizations in June 1994, has definitely set the policy agenda for inclusive education on a global basis. To quote from the Salamanca Statement:

> We the delegates of the World Conference on Special Needs Education...hereby reaffirm our commitment to Education for All, recognising the necessity and urgency of providing education to children, youth, and adults with SEN within the regular education system, and further hereby endorse the Framework for Action on SNE, that governments and organizations may be guided by the spirit of its provisions and recommendations.

Though, in India, there is no formal or official definition of inclusion, it does not only mean the placement of students with SEN in regular classrooms. The Draft Scheme on Inclusive Education prepared by the MHRD uses the following definition: Inclusive education means all learners, young people—with or without disabilities being able to learn together in ordinary preschool provisions, schools, and community educational settings with appropriate network of support services.

Inclusion means the process of educating children with SEN alongside their peers in mainstream schools.

The feasibility of inclusion of such children in schools, however, has been an issue that has been discussed and debated extensively at various national and international fora.

> Inclusion remains a complex and controversial issue which tends to generate heated debates... there is a great deal of uncertainty about the definition of inclusion... it is difficult to find research evidence that can provide definitive guidance as to where policy and practice should be heading.... In this climate some schools express increasing reluctance to admit and retain pupils whose presence could have a negative impact on their overall profile of results...there is a growing movement in education towards differentiated provision—a trend that seems incompatible with an inclusive philosophy.

Benefits of Inclusion for Students without Special Needs

The benefits of inclusion for students with SEN are as follows:

- Spending the school day alongside classmates who do not have disabilities provides many opportunities for social interaction that would not be available in segregated settings.
- Children with SEN have appropriate models of behaviour. They can observe and imitate the socially acceptable behaviour of the students without SEN.
- Teachers often develop higher standards of performance for students with SEN.
- Both general and special educators in inclusive settings expect appropriate conduct from all students.
- Students with SEN are taught age-appropriate, functional components of academic content, which

may never be part of the curriculum in segregated settings (for example, the sciences, social studies, etc.).

- Attending inclusive schools increases the probability that students with SEN will continue to participate in a variety of integrated settings throughout their lives.

Benefits of Inclusion for Students without SEN

The benefits of inclusion for students without SEN are as follows:

- Students without SEN have a variety of opportunities for interacting with peers of their own age who experience SEN, in inclusive school settings.
- They may serve as peer tutors during instructional activities.
- They may play the role of a special "buddy" for the children with SEN during lunch, in the bus, or on the playground.
- Children without SEN can learn a good deal about tolerance, individual difference, and human exceptionality by interacting with those with SEN.
- Children without SEN can learn that students with SEN have many positive characteristics and abilities.
- Children without SEN have the chance to learn about many of the human service professions, such as, special education, speech therapy, physical therapy, recreational therapy, and vocational rehabilitation. For some, exposure to these areas may lead their making a career in any of these areas later on.

- Inclusion offers the opportunity for students without SEN to learn to communicate, and deal effectively with a wide range of individuals. This also prepares them to fully participate in a pluralistic society when they are adults.
- Inclusive education ensures that a school responds to the educational needs of children in the neighbourhood. It brings a school closer to the community.

ISSUES AND CONCERNS OF SPECIAL EDUCATION CURRICULUM

To make inclusive education possible, and to better accommodate students with different learning abilities, the present education system, educational structure, and educational practices need to become more flexible, more inclusive, and more collaborative.

The Purpose

The purpose of inclusive education,

- Is not the same as for a student without SEN—that is, it is not to bring students with SEN up to the level of, or maintain their grades at the same level as, students without SEN.
- It is to meet the individualized goals of students with SEN, within the context of general educational settings and activities.

The following questions need to be addressed while making adaptations to the curriculum. Can a student with SEN participate in the classroom

- Just like his/her classmates?
- With environmental adaptations?
- With instructional adaptations?

- With adapted materials?
- With adapted expectations?

Preschool Programme for Children with SEN

The identification of SEN of children at an early age is crucial to helping them cope with challenges in later life. Thus, the sensitization, orientation, and training of parents, caretakers, and other stakeholders becomes imperative. As per the NSSO, 8.4 per cent and 6.1 per cent of the total estimated households in rural and urban India, respectively, are reported to have at least one disabled person. Therefore, orienting *Anganwadi* and *Balwadi* workers, caregivers, and institutional authorities in early childhood education programmes is highly desirable and needs to be built into the ICDS programme.

The provision of resources and the involvement of the community in identification and intervention in the child's own milieu need emphasis and focus. The benefits of existing knowledge and skills in conjunction with technology can be made to reach the needy through the involvement of local bodies. For example, the Ali Yavar Jung National Institute for Hearing Handicapped (AYJNIHH) has played the role of a catalyst at Badlapur Kulgaon Nagar Palika where the Town Panchayat has resolved to collect Rs. 10 per property per year to help persons with disabilities. As a result, the Town Panchayat collects about Rs.2,25,000 per year through its 22,500 properties. An Apang Samiti, consisting of Persons With Disabilities (PWDs) schools, banks, station masters, post masters, etc. was formed which decides the priorities of the PWDs, including Children with SEN. Empowering the Town Panchayat through a catalyst can be critical for the success of the Early Identification and Intervention Programme. A strong parent/caregiver professional partnership should be developed for the networking and strengthening of intervention programmes.

At the preschool level, a multisensory approach should replace oral and rote learning, facilitate language learning, develop pre-academic skills, and provide for remedial measures in all areas of development. Appropriate diagnostic and remedial assessment should be made available to identify, "at risk" children.

Already developed curriculum packages for preschool children in communication skills, self-help skills, social skills, and specific motor skills may be used. Audio-visual packages for promoting skills in physical, motor, affective, cognitive, and language development of children "at risk" and with SEN may be utilized.

Managing Inclusive Curriculum

Developing inclusive schools that cater to a wide range of pupils in both urban and rural areas requires: the articulation of a clear and forceful policy on inclusion together with adequate financial provision; an effective public information effort to combat prejudice and create informed and positive attitudes; an extensive programme of orientation and staff training; and the provision of necessary support services. Changes in all the following aspects of schooling, as well as many others, are necessary to contribute to the success of inclusive schools: curriculum, buildings, school organization, pedagogy, assessment, staffing, school ethos, and extracurricular activities.

An inclusive curriculum means one curriculum for all students rather than a separate curriculum for students without SEN and another for students with SEN. According to Quinn and Ryba an inclusive curriculum is recognition that under the principle of social justice, participation in education should not involve discrimination on the basis of gender, ethnicity, indigenous group, socio-economic status, and ability or disability. An inclusive curriculum, recognizes the need that schools be organized, with the individual differences of students in mind and allow for scope and flexibility to enable all students to achieve their goals.

Though the National Curriculum Framework for School Education (NCFSE), does mention the education of learners with SEN under the sections "Curriculum Concerns" and "Managing the System", it does not address the SEN of learners under various other sections, such as, "Organization of Curriculum at Elementary and Secondary Stages", "Organization of Curriculum at Higher Secondary Stage", "Evaluation", etc.

Access to Inclusive Curriculum

Booth has pointed out that access to education is only the first stage in overcoming the exclusion of persons with disabilities from the mainstream. More challenging is the task of bringing about a shift in public perspective and values, so that diversity is cherished. However, it is difficult to say whether the first barrier has as yet been overcome in the country.

It is believed that the fundamental right to education will bring more pupils with SEN into ordinary schools, and that this will provide the impetus for change. As stated this will regime a number of innovations in teaching-learning processes, and will also provide pupils with SEN access to a full curriculum in appropriate ways. To facilitate this access, it is important to provide information in Braille, on tape, through sign language, and in simple and straightforward language.

Teaching Practices

In India, the concept of Inclusive Education has not yet been linked to a broader discussion of pedagogy and quality education. Any broad reform in education cannot be implemented without taking the inclusion of learners with SEN into consideration. There are many teachers all over the country who do make small modifications in their teaching in accordance with the principles of inclusive education. The strategies used by them are: group learning, peer tutoring, speaking slowly and clearly, looking at the hearing-impaired child while speaking so that they can lip read, writing on the blackboard, etc. Most teachers are aware of such techniques for classroom management of learners with SEN. In this connection, they often consult the special educator for support.

Work over the last decade has endeavoured to identify specific sub-groups of specific learning difficulties, and there is evidence that it may be valid to distinguish between children with language, visual-spatial, or "mixed processing deficits". However, even if we could make these kinds of distinctions with certainty, there remains the question of how best one can teach these various groups of children. As yet there are no unequivocally "best" methods. Careful monitoring of the child's learning and the encouragement of a broad range of learning strategies remain important characteristics of effective teaching for all children.

Content Areas

The goals of education are the same for all children provided that these goals are balanced and brought in harmony with the individual needs of each child. It is important to institute conversational domains in planning curricula. In schools these domains have been pre-established and take the form of disciplines such as language, mathematics, social studies, and science. A more appropriate emphasis might be domains that are culturally specific and imbue a natural facilitation for conversation centred around "living traditions". In order to accomplish this end, participation is key and students are actually "doing" science or social studies instead of simply reading or being told about them.

The SEN may emanate from a number of reasons. Not all children with disabilities have SEN at the elementary level. They learn along with their peers with the help of aids such as wheelchairs, hearing aids, optical or non-optical aids, educational aids like Taylor frames, the abacus, etc. However, there may be students who may require the following:

- Additional time and a suitable mode for the successful completion of tests.
- Modification, substitution, and disapplication of the curriculum because it presents specific difficulties for them.
- Provision of adapted, modified, or alternative activities in different content areas.
- Accessible texts and materials to suit their ages and levels of learning;
- Appropriate management of classrooms (for example, management of noise, glare, etc.)
- Provision of additional support by using ICT or video.

Inclusion is all about providing effective learning opportunities to all students. Therefore, it depends on whether teachers modify the National Curriculum programmes of study whenever necessary in order to provide relevant and challenging work to students. It means being flexible and choosing content from a lower level or higher level if necessary. There may be students who may perform below the expected level. For these students a greater degree of differentiation may be necessary. On the other hand, students whose performances exceed those of others within one or more subjects may need suitably challenging work. What is important is that no matter how they learn or perform, they should experience success and not failure.

Many suggestions in different domain areas were given when interviewing teachers teaching in classrooms where children with SEN were studying along with other children. They have been broadly summarized as follows:

Mathematics

To overcome access difficulties to learning mathematics, some pupils may require help in interpreting the data in graphs, tables, or bar charts. Some may require access to tactile, and others to specialist, equipment for work related to shape, geometry, calculations, etc. They may also require more time to complete their work. There may be some who may require simpler language or more pictures and need help in interpreting oral directions, while making mental calculations. Use of ICT may be required to overcome difficulties in quantitative and abstract thinking.

Language

Some pupils may have specific difficulties in learning languages and may require help in improving their areas of weaknesses and in devising strategies to overcome their difficulties. There may be some children who may require alternative communication systems to compensate for the difficulties hey face in using spoken language. Lele and Khaledkar found that children having problems in hearing had difficulty in language comprehension when instructed with the language textbook prescribed for the general class. These children with special needs required a greater number of periods to learn the content. Paranjpe reported significant differences in achievement of language skills between children with and without hearing impairment, the former being deficient in language skills. Children having difficulties in writing may need to make use of ICT, while there may be some who may require opportunities to learn and develop a tactile method of interpreting written information. Content related to real-life situations would benefit all children.

Remedial programmes in language would be effective in improving the reading comprehension of all children including those having reading disorders. The use of computer-based remedial strategies have been reported as having yielded a 5 per cent improvement in the performance of children with specific learning disabilities in Mathematics and a 7 per cent improvement in English.

Sign language and Braille may find a place in the three language formula in school education, and this would not only help students with SEN in language learning, but also create awareness and sensitivity amongst children without SEN.

Science

In learning science, some students may require support with mobility or manipulation skills to participate in experiments being performed both indoors and outdoors. Students can benefit from adapted or alternative activities, adapted equipment, the use of ICT, adult or peer support, additional time, and support in lessons that may not be accessible to them because of their impairment.

Social studies

In order to gain access to this subject, some students may require support in the form of prepared tapes to access text; help in writing to communicate their ideas through alternative communication methods such as ICT or speech; adaptation of content and activities; education aids to manage visual information; and/or support to understand various geographical concepts and features and the environment.

Group activities such as projects and assignments done through cooperative learning will enable students with SEN to participate actively in all classroom activities.

Art, Craft and Music

Art is a very effective medium of self-expression and communication. It provides a number of media such as dance, drama, music, painting, sculpture, carving, puppetry, etc. for self-expression and communication with the world, and helps in developing self-confidence and self-worth in learners. Art classes may also encourage many students to take up this creative mode of self-expression as their profession in future life. For students with SEN, art education also acts as a healthy leisure activity. To gain access to these areas students may require alternative activities/opportunities, additional time, etc.

Health, Hygiene, Yoga, Sports and Physical Education

These curricular components are important for students with SEN and improve the following:

- Personal health and physical development
- Movement concepts and motor skills
- Mental health including peace
- Relationships with other people

Studies and experiments have indicated that most of the children with disabilities can play a number of games without any support or special effort. Little effort is needed to make the games adapted to children with visual and multiple disabilities. Children with orthopaedic disabilities could also do the *yogasans* (yogic postures/exercises. Available research evidence also reveals that music, dance, and *yogasans* have a therapeutic effect on children with mental retardation, and have helped improve their attention and concentration

Work Education

Work education provides students with SEN studying at the secondary level an opportunity to understand the world of work and readies them for possible future careers. Obviously, everyone has to earn his/her livelihood by employment in appropriate work. The curriculum should provide for proper career counselling and also for training in pre-vocational skills. The pre-vocational skills include acquisition of work skills, awareness of work ethics, appropriate work habits, and responsibility sharing. Pre-vocational skills training should also include development and inculcation of values such as honesty, punctuality, dignity of labour, respect for teamwork, and productivity consciousness. Students with SEN may take more time to adjust to the work setting, the work environment, their colleagues, and also to the idea of money management. Liaising between the world of work and education will also provide an opportunity to the employer to observe and suggest further improvements. This can also be an opportunity for students with SEN to get absorbed or to get selected for jobs while studying. This interface between the world of work and education will also help in changing the attitude of people in general and in creating awareness in society about students with SEN. In order to bring about effective liaising between the world of work and education, the curriculum should be in proper harmony with the demands and needs of the industry. In other words, the mainstream school curriculum should provide the facility of vocational streaming.

Students with SEN at the secondary and senior secondary level of schooling can be properly guided for a particular vocation in accordance with their abilities, aptitudes, and interest. The training required should be arranged as far as possible within the school compound or at a centre near the place of residence. The monitoring, follow-up, funding, and evaluation of the training should be the joint responsibility of the immediate family, the institution, government personnel, the NGOs, and the Panchayats.

Evaluation

The NCFSE was critical of the present evaluation system. Teachers regard the mainstream as curriculum-oriented and examination-driven, with pressures of high achievement. Teaching in India stands subordinated to examination and not examination to teaching. Thus, the focus is on the completion of a rigid and vast curriculum.

Collaborative forms of assessment for inclusive classrooms is a good idea. Collaboration between, and consultation with, the student, parents, caregivers, and other relevant people enable educators to gain a good understanding of the students' strengths and needs. The difference between traditional assessment methods and collaborative forms of assessment are shown in Table 1.

Flexible strategies for assessment and accreditation have been recommended by the *Open File on Inclusive Education* ((UNESCO). Appropriate assessment enables,

- Students who are talented and gifted to move at their natural learning pace.
- Students who progress more slowly than their peers to move at their own pace whilst still being part of the content of themes and lessons.

- Students experiencing specific learning problems to receive creative and effective support to maximize their success.

The open file gives examples from various countries with the following strategies:

- They break or weaken the link between assessment and progression.
- They relate assessment to broad objectives on which the curriculum is based rather than to the making of specified content.
- They develop flexible forms of accreditation.

Table 1. Difference between traditional assessment methods and collaborative forms of assessment

Traditional Assessment	*Collaborative Assessment*
Based on a medical model	Based on an ecological model
Focuses on deficits within the student	Focuses on abilities, strengths, and needs of the student
Assessment procedures are unrelated to the curriculum	Assessment procedures are related to the and learning context curriculum and context of learning
Hierarchical expect model—there is inequality	Team members are seen as equal in human between the student and the 'examiner' dignity
One-shot assessment approach	Assessment is a continuous process
Student is viewed as passive recipient of assessment	Student is viewed as active participant and collaborator
Focus is on the learning products or outcomes	Focus is on the learning process and achievements of the student
The assessment is carried out by a specialist	Parents and other relevant people are working in isolation consulted and involved in the assessment.

Resources

Many students with SEN either go to regular schools or to special schools for education. There are others who, because of the severity of their conditions, are educated at home through community-based rehabilitation services. Finally, there may be some children enrolled in open learning or non-formal or alternative systems of education. Wherever children are enrolled, the crucial issue in the development practices is to meet the educational needs of children and this requires resources. The need for resources to facilitate effective teaching may vary from school to school. However, it is generally believed by teachers that they definitely require the resource support of a special educator to assist them in providing equal opportunities to students with SEN.

Other resources being used in mainstream schools include collaboration with special schools existing nearby. One very good example of this is the National Association For The Blind, an NGO, which runs a special school cum resource centre. This NGO has its branches all over the country. Not only does it provide residential facilities for students with visual disabilities right from a very young age, but it also integrates them in the general education system whenever it is appropriate for the child. It also provides resource support to the child throughout the school years and helps him/her in gaining access to the curriculum.

Staff Development

The effectiveness of the curriculum depends, in the long run, on the skills and attitudes of classroom teachers. *The Open File on Inclusive Education* suggests that the following demands be placed on teachers from the perspective of inclusive curricula:

— They have to become involved in curriculum development at the local level, and they have to be skilled in curriculum adaptation in their own classrooms.

- They have to manage a complex range of classroom activities.
- They have to know how to support their students' learning without giving them predetermined answers.
- They have to work outside traditional subject boundaries and in culturally sensitive ways.

The willingness of teachers to include children with SEN in the general class depend on the children's disabling conditions. Teachers should have positive attitudes towards some children with specific disabilities like visual and hearing disabilities. Attitudes should least positive towards the intellectually impaired and those with behavioural problems.

At present, there are no specific provisions in the form of trained teacher educators, resource materials, and standardized inputs on learners with SEN in the in-service programmes of the DIETs. In the pre-service programme, only one optional paper or one unit in a compulsory paper are the inputs provided. Training programmes under DPEP, and now the SSA, cover this component, but it needs to be strengthened and made more relevant to the needs of the teachers from the perspective of inclusive education.

CHALLENGES AHEAD

For years the education system has provided special education and related services to students with SEN and systematically developed a dual service delivery system comprising different settings, different curricula, different services, and different service providers for students with and without SEN. But now in the context of the struggle to affirm and guarantee the rights of the disabled, the ethics of the dual system are being questioned. The common system, which would bring "all" onto a common platform, is being thought of as a better option. It is, therefore, important to bring about a number of reforms at various levels in order to develop a "school for all" having an inclusive curriculum. The curriculum needs to be balanced in such a way that it is common for all, and yet takes account of the individual needs of all learners. It is also important to take into consideration pedagogical issues. The curriculum should be accessible to all children and for this specialist support would be required. Care then has to be exercised to ensure that learners with SEN are not segregated from the mainstream by providing this specialist support. How the school organizes itself to be an effective school that takes care of the individual needs of all pupils is another issue to be considered. While being flexible in the timetable and delivery of the curriculum, the school should also provide for the resource support needed in the form of special educators, assistive devices, and teaching-learning material.

The professional development of teachers and educators is an important issue and must incorporate attitudinal change, and the knowledge and skills necessary to lead to an inclusive society. Finally, no initiative towards inclusive education would be complete without collaborating with parents and without the external support of NGOs and special schools for providing inputs on training, curriculum delivery, assessment, etc.

2

STATE OF INCLUSIVE EDUCATION

A focus on disability in global development not only raises questions of diverse local interpretations of the same issue, but also the need to accept the diversity of needs within this 'group' depending on both the nature of impairment and cultural context. The linguistic translation, let alone personal understanding, of new, often 'northern', terminologies and ideas can be problematic, and the English word 'disability' does not escape this conceptual tension. In this light, it is useful to outline models and definitions of 'disability' which are in use.

The medical model defines disability scientifically, as a physical, medically-diagnozed deficit which handicaps. It is impairment-focused, isolating the experience of disability from external influences such as societal attitudes. In India, the Ministry of Social Justice and Empowerment, which is responsible for people with disabilities, has a medically-inspired classification system whereby one's disability either falls into the category of locomotor, visual, hearing, speech or mental. These broad categorizations cannot demonstrate the extent or exact type of impairment, which could assist in assessment of medical, and in some cases educational, need, and have no bearing on the social aspects of disablement, perhaps reflecting cultural perceptions of what 'disability' means in India.

In most northern discourses the social model has overtaken the medical model, whereby cultural environment and attitudes which influence disabled people's societal participation and citizenship status are seen as the handicap, rather than the physical impairment. Hence it has a more human rights, as well as contextual, dimension. While the social model is salient in all contexts, it ignores the significance of the type and extent of impairment at the expense of highlighting the socio-political aspects.

The United Kingdom Department for International Development (DFID) appears to neatly combine both the medical and social models in its definition of disability as: "...long term impairment leading to social and economic disadvantages, denial of rights, and limited opportunities to play an equal part in the life of the community." This definition both combines health and social implications, and includes human rights and social exclusion dimensions in this complex, supposedly catch-all word 'disability'. However, it could be argued that in order to be applicable to all situations, this definition is 'fuzzy' and so not very useful when it comes to ascertaining the extent and types of need, because varied definitions of 'disability' have an impact on the data available on its existence and prevalence. Hence, although variation is implied in the broadness of the definition, it is important to be aware of the extent to which cultural context can influence not only data collection and provision, but also how a person with disabilities experiences both their impairment and handicapping environment.

DISABILITY—AN ISSUE FOR DEVELOPMENT

The World Health Organization (WHO) estimates that 10 per cent of any population are disabled. In addition, approximately 85 per cent of the world's children with disabilities under 15 live in developing countries. It is further thought that with disability, or impairment, being both a cause and consequence of poverty, the Millennium Development Goals cannot be achieved without a specific disability focus. People with disabilities have health, nutritional, educational and gender needs too, yet the goals related to these issues currently ignore the often unique needs of people with disabilities within these goals.

The WHO estimates that up to 50 per cent of disabilities are preventable, with 70 per cent of blindness and 50 per cent of hearing impairment in children in developing countries being preventable or treatable. Although this can be seen as more of a health issue than a disability politics one, its link to healthcare, malnutrition and poverty makes disability a development issue.

Disabled children are more likely to die young, or be neglected, malnourished and poor, while the denial of education can lead to a lack of employment opportunities and so poverty. Similarly, poverty can lead to malnutrition, dangerous working and living conditions bad health and maternity care, poor sanitation, and vulnerability to natural disasters—all of which can result in disability. This vicious cycle of poverty and disability is demonstrated in Figure 1. Seen in this light, it is hard to deny a strong link between poverty and disability, although it is important to be aware of other contributing factors such as lack of, or badly implemented, social policies that may lead to these conditions in the first place.

There is a growing consensus that people with disabilities should be included in development programmes, as the exclusion to date of this marginalized group will probably result in the non-achievement of the

UN Millennium Commission's broadly inclusive global development agenda. However, if a person with a disability is dehumanized by cultural belief or stigma, as they are in India, then they can be 'invisibilized' and not considered worthy of rights. Disability is clearly a development issue that we ignore at a price, including that of human rights.

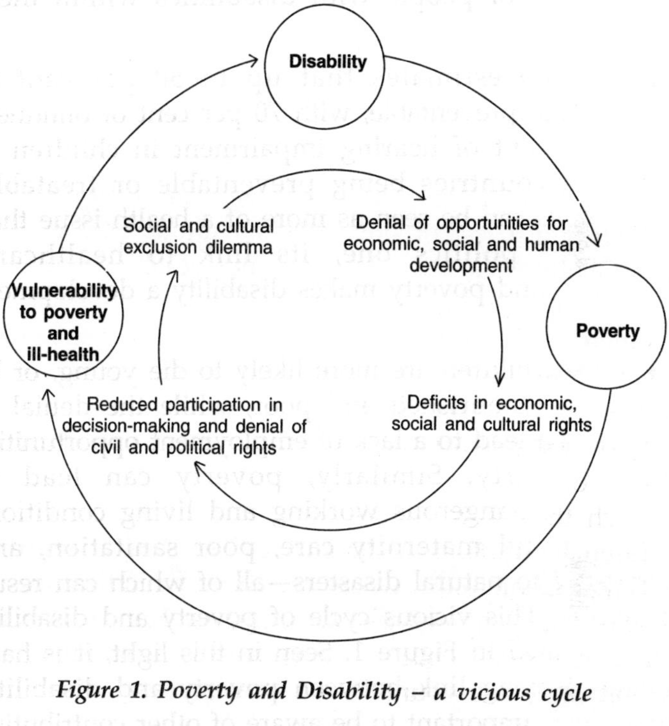

Figure 1. Poverty and Disability – a vicious cycle

EDUCATION FOR ALL (EFA) AND CHILDREN WITH DISABILITIES

There are as many as 1 in 10 children with special needs in education in the world. However, it is worth noting that children with special educational needs (e.g. dyslexia) will outnumber those with visible impairments, again raising the issue of multiple understandings and definitions of what exactly disability is. Despite the accuracy issues surrounding the sporadic and varied collection of data on disability, the fact that estimated enrolment rates of children with disabilities vary between less than 1 per cent to 3 per cent is hard to ignore. Deon Filmer, while questioning the validity of sample sizes and survey methods used in his survey of 11 countries, found that although disability may not always be directly linked to poverty, "...disability among youth is ... systematically and significantly related to lower school participation".

Not only is lack of access to schooling a violation of Article 28 of the UN Convention on the Rights of the Child, which states the right of all children to free primary education, but this lack also potentially maintains the cycle of poverty, as without education an educationally excluded adult may not be able to work to earn a living, or participate in political processes. Despite this, there is no indicator in the Education For All (EFA) Global Monitoring Reports for enrolment, drop-out, or attainment of disabled children. In fact, there is no disability indicator at all, which is potentially excluding millions of children from a high-profile global campaign in which they were vaguely included in the category of "children in difficult circumstances" in EFA goal two at the Dakar Conference, where the drive for Education For All was finally agreed by 92 countries. Hence, although EFA is about 'all' children, it appears that children with disabilities do not count in the final analysis.

WHAT IS INCLUSIVE EDUCATION (IE)?

Until recently, most conceptual literature on inclusive education was Northern in origin, taking a 'whole-school' approach to institutional change, and influenced by the social model of disability. Children in special schools were seen as geographically and socially segregated from their peers, and the initial movement to locationally integrate these students in mainstream schools shifted to one where the whole school was encouraged to become more adaptable and inclusive in its day-to-day educational practices for all students. Pedagogy in particular was highlighted as the key to meeting all students' educational needs by making the curriculum flexible, and so more accessible.

By recognizing that teaching methods which can make curriculum accessible to children with disabilities can also make learning accessible to all students, a teacher or school principal is well on the way to improving the overall quality of their school. In this way, inclusive education is not a disability-only issue, but an educational quality issue.

There is a growing, although not comprehensive, literature in the south, which focuses more on external factors with its 'community approach'. In developing contexts with large numbers of out-of-school children, inclusive education tends to be more broadly concerned with school access and education deprivations for marginalized groups such as girls, ethnic minorities, poor families and disabled children, who have never attended or dropped out of school.

It seems that there is currently an expanding discourse on inclusive education developing amongst some academics and teaching professionals in India, many of whom see inclusive education as exclusively concerned with children with disabilities. This discourse is attempting to shift perceptions of disability from the medical model to the social model. However, there are many conceptual difficulties with the terms of integration and inclusion in India, which are often used interchangeably. Further, varying definitions of disability and subjective interpretations of what 'type' of child a teacher is willing to include in their classroom add to the confusion.

Even if a previously excluded child is given access to a mainstream classroom, what happens within that space can be anything but inclusive if the school quality is poor, they cannot access an inflexible curriculum, or they are ignored or bullied by the teacher or their peers. It is worth noting that the concept of inclusive education in the mainstream as opposed to specialist segregated provision is a matter of heated, inconclusive debate in the North, and yet it is seemingly being transferred unquestioningly as the panacea to the exclusion of children with disabilities in the South.

While in northern contexts, the discourse around inclusive education is primarily concerned with segregation as opposed to inclusion in the mainstream, in the south the coverage of special schools is so limited that the discourse is concerned with inclusion being potentially the most cost and time-efficient way of improving access to educational institutions. It may be that the promotion by the World Bank and OECD of the cost-effectiveness of inclusion in the mainstream enabling both economic and social benefits may bear more relevance for resource-constrained governments and policy-makers than a child-rights approach.

MERGING AGENDAS

Disability is not only closely related to poverty, but is also becoming widely recognized as a cross-cutting development issue that bears relevance to all dimensions of social exclusion. Although social exclusion is not necessarily the opposite of inclusion, the extensive literature that is fast developing around processes of social exclusion can potentially assist in our understanding of combinations of exclusionary dimensions. Factors such as gender, ethnicity, disability, and poverty are rarely experienced exclusively, and as such are mutually reinforcing. Processes such as inclusive education could meet the needs of students affected by any of these dimensions. Social exclusion frameworks go some way towards understanding the processes involved and their intersecting nature. For example, women with disabilities are two to three times more likely to be victims of physical and sexual abuse than those without, demonstrating how being a woman and disabled can lead to double discrimination. In addition, more boys with disabilities go to school than girls with disabilities, and people with disabilities are usually the poorest of the poor.

Lack of education is often attributed to poverty rather than policy, because exposing poor policy choices puts a spotlight on abuses of power. Indeed, power hierarchies are a key determinant of social exclusion, although poverty, policy, quality and relevance of education available, and stakeholder attitudes all have essential roles to play too in a family's decision, or ability, to send a child to school. While it is important to see disability in the context of other dimensions of social exclusion, The deficits associated with disability are large compared to other sources of inequality, such as gender, rural/urban disparities, and wealth. Disability is different from other forms of disadvantage because people with disabilities cannot organize or mobilize until their practical needs, such as mobility aids, are met, and they cannot fight for their rights until they are more empowered.

SIZE AND DIVERSITY OF DISABLED CHILDREN

India has the second largest education system in the world, with 200 million children aged between 6 and 14, around 25 million of whom are out of school. However, bearing in mind that apparently only 35 per cent of children are registered at birth, others estimate between 35 to 80 million out-of-school children.

When considering understandings of, approaches to, and impacts of inclusive education, the inevitable diversity and complexity in a context of this size must be taken into account. India's 1.3 billion people speak 18 different languages, and 844 dialects, worship varied religions, have unique customs, differ in their exposure to disease and access to types of nutrition which affect their health and socio-economic status, and also communications which influence their access to government resources such as education or healthcare.

This diversity is further reflected in disparities of educational achievement. For example, in Kerala the literacy rate recorded in the 2001 Census was 90.92 per cent, while in Bihar it was 47.53 per cent. As a result, the overall (average) literacy rate for India was 65.38 per cent which, while a representative figure is a national aggregate and so cannot reflect the complexity of context. However, it is worth noting that about 40 per cent of India's population lives in the educationally worst performing states, suggesting that a significant proportion of Indians are under-served by their education systems. Added to this issue of averaging out statistics in such a vast country is the fact that when census data was collected, there were some areas which were cut off by "disturbances" or "natural calamaties" such as the Kashmiri conflict, floods or landslides. This shows how despite best intentions, there may be unsurveyed people whose issues are therefore invisible to policy-makers, and so they perhaps do not have access to government resources.

Data on children with disabilities seems to be as unreliable as other figures, perhaps due to Filmer's "selective reporting" of obvious physical impairments, or children being hidden by their families out of shame. A basic disability statistic was recently included in the 2001 Census for the first time, as a result of campaigning by the Indian disability movement.

Despite there being no disability indicators in the influential EFA Global Monitoring Reports, the addition of this disability statistic may indicate the positive influence of the introduction of the inclusive education concept. The census finding of a 2.2 per cent disabled population, or 21,906,769, are challenged by NGOs in the field who believe the figure to be closer to 6 per cent, or 70 million.

In India, disability is measured in five categories—sight, speech, hearing, locomotor, and mental—which excludes disabilities such as autism. In addition, a person has to be medically certified as having 40 per cent or more of one of these disabilities in order to be counted and so qualified to request 'benefits'. This seems to leave the ticking of census/survey boxes wide open to subjective interpretation, and perhaps even the gaining of disability certificates open to corruption. Whatever the true figure, it is worth noting that according to the 2002 National Sample Survey, only 45 per cent of the disabled population is literate, and 9 per cent has secondary level education or higher. Importantly, although perceptions of disability for data collection may vary from State to State, the fact that this data is now being collected is a step towards raising awareness and could develop into a wider understanding of disability and broader exclusion issues over time.

PERCEPTIONS OF DISABILITY

Although from a northern perspective disability might be described in terms of a combination of impairment and social barriers, "the WHO manual states explicitly that valuation depends on cultural norms,". Hence, it is important to present here a brief outline of Indian societal perceptions of disability in order to gain some insight into the cultural context in which the concept of inclusive education is interpreted and implemented.

It appears that in India the medical model of disability, with its often accompanying attitude of within-child (or adult) deficit, applies as the cultural norm. Disability can also be seen as having value as a source of income in Hindu India as the deficit, whatever it may be, entitles the disabled person to the charity and mercy of others, and so qualifies them for the job of begging. However, this anthropologically empathetic view does not take into account the potentially disempowering effects of being a passive recipient of welfare.

In "Responding to difference: Policies to support 'inclusive education' in India", a paper presented at the Inclusive and Supportive Education Congress 2005, Singal, N. points out how the individualization of disability in India as a personal, inherent problem of mind and body reinforces the image of a problem to be diagnozed and cured so a person can be more 'normal'. This, Singal argues, results in the charity and welfare focus on aids and appliances to assist those with disabilities to be 'normalized'. This view does not address the fact that in an environment lacking such helpful hardware, this focus may be justified. However, Singal does point out that the dominance of this medical perspective may be a result of many disabilities in India being the consequence of poor health and nutrition, and limited access to immunization programmes.

According to UNICEF only 60 per cent of women receive antenatal care, 43 per cent are assisted by a skilled attendant at delivery, and 30 per cent of children are not immunized against polio. Cramped and dangerous living and working conditions are also preventable causes of much disability. These "disabling conditions", which are prevalent in many developing countries, are a key reason for the dominance of the medical model at the expense of awareness or exploration of the social dimensions of disablement deemed so influential in the North. Similarly, the pity shown towards disabled people, who may be seen as suffering for the sins of their past life, so that those giving 'charity' can improve their own *karma* for the next, enables Indian society to remain ignorant of its own role in building disabling barriers. However, with only an estimated 100,000 of perhaps 15 million children with disabilities catered for in existing institutions, "charity cannot cope".

Singal explains how the notion of distributive justice is prevalent in all social welfare efforts to advance Scheduled Caste (SC), Scheduled Tribe (ST), and Other Backward Castes (OBCs) in post-independence India, for example through government job reservation, and that this is similarly reflected in the approach to disability. The positive discrimination of job allocation perpetuates the caste system because the job is given on the basis of caste, or disability, and not on merit.

Caste, and the more 'modern' mobile socio-economic notion of class, has a key role to play in power processes at national and local levels, including educational access within school and classroom. Dalits, make up over 50 per cent of the population who are outside the caste system, excluded from the higher echelons of mainstream society structured according to caste. While there may appear to be hope of social mobility in the first generation of Dalit learners entering formal schooling, which is dominated by upper-caste teachers, parental aspirations of a reserved government job have been found in recent empirical research to be tempered by the security of a 'realistic fallback' option of caste-specific work. In the case of children with disabilities, this may well be begging.

Where do people with disabilities fit into this social system? Some see the disabled as a fifth caste, below all others—impure and so not 'whole' which may contribute to their societal invisiblization in surveys and censi. In addition, the strong link between poverty and disability implies that many children with disabilities will be members of Dalit families, perhaps reinforcing their marginalization. While impairment is not restricted to any one class or age group, people with disabilities are often found to be amongst the poorest of the poor. However, a caste/disability link doesn't seem to have been empirically researched to date in the Indian context.

There are many government and NGO programmes focused on caste and gender in India, yet none yet seem to be concerned with how disability interacts and reinforces these dimensions of exclusion. For example, the multiple handicap of being a disabled woman can manifest itself in many ways. Her marriage chances are slight, she may be more subject to infanticide, her dowry higher because she is perceived as infertile, she is more likely to be abused or hidden from public view by her family, and she ceases to exist as a person and is excluded from being recognized as a woman in the fullest sense because she does not fit in with the model of women defined by society and dear to the collective imagination. These societal and cultural assumptions surrounding women with disabilities are added to by the worship of female beauty and perfection in an Indian media which wields great power in a widely illiterate population. If a girl-child is perceived as unmarriageable and unable to do domestic chores, then in some eyes she is not deemed worthy of the education which could potentially give her economic freedom and societal status. It is important to recognize, however, that for some parents the likelihood that their daughter may not marry leads them to see education and training as essential in order to give her financial independence.

CONCEPTS OF INCLUSIVE EDUCATION

Although it may not be appropriate to judge the adoption of a northern concept in the South from a northern perspective, hasty use of such globalized terminology without engaging with the thinking behind it may present no more than empty rhetoric, whatever the context. Inclusive education is a concept that has been adopted from the international discourse, but has not been engaged with in the Indian scenario.

Indian understandings of disability and educational needs are demonstrated through the interchangeable use of several English terms which hold different meanings in the North. For example, children with special needs or special educational needs tend to be perceived as children with disabilities in India. In contrast, the intention of Mary Warnock's term 'special educational needs', coined in the UK in 1978, was to imply that any child, with an impairment or not, may have an individual educational need at some point in their school career which the teacher should adapt to. This further implies that a child with a disability may not have a special educational need while their able-bodied peers could.

In addition, despite the 1987 Mental Health Act finally separating the meaning of learning disability from that of mental illness in India, there is still some confusion in understanding, with the 1995 Persons with Disabilities Act listing both mental retardation and mental illness as categories of disability. Ignorance and fear of genetic inheritance adds to the societal stigma of both. 'Inclusive' and 'integrated' education are also concepts that are used interchangeably, understood as the placement of children with disabilities in mainstream classrooms, with the provision of aids and appliances, and specialist training for the teacher on how to 'deal with' students with disabilities. There is little engagement with the connotations of school, curriculum, and teacher flexibility for all children. These rigid, categorical interpretations of subtly different northern concepts are perhaps a reflection of not only the government tendency to categorize and label but also a cultural one, most explicitly enforced through the rigidly categorized caste system.

While it is easy to criticize the apparent lack of critical engagement with these terms in India, this is perhaps a reflection of the weakness of local Disabled People's Organizations' (DPOs) political voice which have had such an overt influence on the development of these concepts in the north. It may also reflect an unwillingness to engage with an understanding of social exclusion and the, "...barriers to entry and participation in the education system faced by children due to reasons other than impairment". However, it is worth noting that this political discourse has a 40 year plus history in the North, while it is relatively new in the South.

IMPLEMENTATION OF IE PROGRAMMES

This section will explore the implementation of government, NGO, and private school IE programmes before examining educational policy and its accompanying issues and constraints for children with disabilities in India.

Government Programmes

Over the years, although government programmes such as Operation Blackboard and Lok Jumbish focused mainly on infrastructure, girls, scheduled caste and scheduled tribe children, others had, or have, inclusive education components which ensure the visibility of children with disabilities.

Integrated Education for Disabled Children (IEDC)

The Ministry of Welfare, now Social Justice and Empowerment, implemented the Integrated Education for Disabled Children (IEDC) scheme from 1974 to 1982, when it transferred to the Department of Education. The scheme was apparently intended to encourage co-operation between mainstream and special schools in order to support integration. The programme is seen as an overall failure by those outside the government. IEDC has been replaced by the Integrated Education for the Disabled (IED) component of the national District Primary Education Project (DPEP), and supports community mobilization and early detection, in-service teacher training, architectural design in schools, the establishment of resource centres, teacher training, identification and assessment of children with disabilities, and the supply of specialist aids and appliances.

Project on Integrated Education for Disabled (PIED)

In 1987, UNICEF and the government-funded National Council of Educational Research and Training (NCERT) launched the Project on Integrated Education for Disabled (PIED) in 10 blocks, that focused on teacher training in order to encourage integration. PIED was later amalgamated with the DPEP and SSA and by 2002 extended to 27 States.

While enrolment of children with disabilities in the mainstream increased and retention was high, coverage has been "miniscule" with only 2-3 per cent of children with disabilities integrated in mainstream institutions. Criticisms made in the project evaluation pointed to implementation issues, such as children getting financial assistance who were not classified as disabled, or teacher training courses being un-regulated. However, the design of the project which encouraged continued labelling of children and withdrawal of those with disabilities from particular activities in school was not highlighted. Further, despite aiming to deliver learner-centred teacher training courses, much of the course instruction was found to be traditionally formal hence failing in one of its key objectives of instigating change in pedagogy through teacher training.

District Primary Education Programme (DPEP)

The 1995 District Primary Education Programme (DPEP), funded 85 per cent by Central Government via a World Bank loan and support from the European Community, UNICEF and the UK and Netherlands governments, and 15 per cent by the State governments, focused on the universalization of primary education, particularly for girls. The intention was for district-specific planning to make the programme contextual, and for participatory processes to empower and build capacity at all levels. However, the programme focused on quantitative targets and educational administration capacity-building more than participation, hence failing to empower local communities, unlike Lok Jumbish. Children with disabilities were included with the aim of achieving EFA. Extensive construction led to the creation of 200,000 new schools, and a teacher-training component led to the in-service training of all teachers. There were failures not so willingly reported such as corruption in the form of budgets for non-existent non-formal education centres, tribal dropout, the difficulty of multigrade teaching in one-teacher schools, low learning achievement, and no integration for children with disabilities due to continued reliance on special school systems. However, it is arguable that the existence of special school systems does not necessarily obstruct locational integration in the mainstream.

Janshala

This community schools programme, started in 1998 and now replaced by SSA, was a collaboration between the Government of India and the UNDP, UNICEF, UNESCO, the ILO, and UNFPA, and supported the government drive towards universal primary education. It covered 120, mainly rural, blocks in 9 States where there is evidence of low female literacy, child labour, and SC/ST children not catered for under DPEP. Unfortunately, due to limited availability of data, it is not possible to elaborate on any issues arising on the *Janshala* programme, which has a component designed to improve the attendance of difficult to reach groups of children, including children with disabilities.

Sarva Shiksha Abhiyan (SSA)

Sarva Shiksha Abhiyan (SSA) is the government's millennial Education For All umbrella programme for all education schemes, which aims to universalize elementary education. The goals are that all children aged 6-14

- *(i)* will be in some form of education by 2003,
- *(ii)* will complete 5 years' primary education by 2007, and
- *(iii)* will complete 8 years' education by 2010.

Disability indicators are included in the government agreement for SSA, although what exactly these are and whether they are taken on at local level is unclear. In fact, although one of the official SSA objectives is the enrolment of children with disabilities, the World Bank SSA project appraisal does not list disability as a key indicator, unlike gender, SC and ST.

The fact that there are still many children out-of-school in 2006 demonstrates not only how behind this programme already is, but also how over-ambitious the infrastructure-led SSA goals were in the first place. For example, of the 1 million new classrooms that should have been built by 2007, there are only 300,000; 100,000 of which are not fully functional. Part of the "compelling" rationale for World Bank assistance to SSA was the continuous monitoring and evaluation and the built-in accountability mechanism at the school and community levels. With donor support of the government feedback system, it was hoped that, the development of mechanisms to assure cross-state and cross district observation, dialogue, and learning for programme refinement could be among SSA's most enduring features. However, despite an awareness of SSA lagging so far behind in the achievement of its intended targets, there is apparently no sign of accelerated political momentum to lend a sense of urgency to the task.

With a planned central: state government budget ratio of 85:15 changing to 50:50 in 2007, there is a high risk of some states not being able to afford to finance the programme, and perhaps an accompanying weakening of political will and programme implementation. The lack of political voice of the poorest people this programme is intended to assist, further pushes education to the lower strata of politicians' agendas. While criticism from the Indian media may be justified and necessary to raise awareness, it remains to be seen whether SSA will be able to adapt and become more effective over the next four years.

NGO Programmes

There are many international, national, and local NGOs involved with disability issues in India. Many local NGOs, while diverse and widespread, tend to be based on a charity/welfare approach and informed by the medical model. Although the exact number is unknown, there are at least 1,000 NGOs and voluntary organizations actively engaged in education, of which the government funded 701 with grants in aid in 2004-5.

NGOs are perceived by the government as widening the implementation network and bringing flexibility and innovation into education programmes. In fact, they are currently implementing much of the IEDC scheme, as the job of including children with disabilities in education nationwide is too vast for the government to be able to undertake alone. (NGOs) "are important stakeholders in social development programmes...[and] are also a repository of knowledge of grassroots realities because of their proximity to the people".

While demonstrating an awareness of the advantage of NGOs' closeness to the people, there is no hint of criticism of the government not being so, or why. In fact, it seems to assume and accept government distance in a nation of hierarchies. While failing to criticize the power processes that make the government need grassroot NGO assistance in the first place, this can also be understood as a pragmatic, honest approach, with the government admitting its failings and resource constraints by embracing NGOs.

Many national and local NGOs support special institutions, perhaps because it is easier to raise public support for residential centres than the promotion of inclusive education. However, a NGO that combines both specialist and inclusive aims is the National Association for the Blind (NAB). With branches nationwide, the NAB facilitates integration with skill and resource support. While it can be criticized for its roots in the medical model, it is important to remember that the specialist support they provide can assist with literacy and mobility for the mainstream classroom and beyond.

Some NGOs have metamorphozed their specialist institutions into resource centres in order to support inclusive education. For example, the Spastics Society of India (SSI) advocates for better understanding that many children with cerebral palsy do not have learning disabilities. The head office has also become a 'National Resource Centre for Inclusion' for all children marginalized from learning, including girls and working children, operating inclusive pre-school classrooms in Mumbai's slum areas. In addition, they offer a postgraduate diploma in inclusive education among other courses, in order to clarify this much-misunderstood concept. However, SSI's impact is currently mostly limited to the cities of Mumbai, Bangluru and Chennai. Similarly, the Jesuit-run Divine Light Trust for the Blind near Bangluru has become a resource centre to train teachers in mainstream schools in order to encourage the inclusion of blind children in their classrooms.

International NGOs too have a role to play in the promotion of inclusive education. Some, such as Voluntary Service Overseas (VSO) and Action on Disability and Development (ADD), both DFID-funded, focus on advocacy through civil society movements. Save the Children UK (SCUK) operates in several states in northern India through local NGOs, with a focus on child rights. They fund, for example, the Society for the Integrated Development of the Himalayas (SIDH) which has successfully supported the establishment of innovative community schools in remote mountain areas with scattered tribal populations and lack of physical access to government schools due to the local terrain. While SIDH has had a positive impact on the inclusion of girls and tribal children in education, they do not appear to have encountered children with disabilities in any of the villages where they work.

SCUK's international policy decision to look at all aspects of exclusion from education together, without specification, may assist in the gradual adoption of a schools-for-all understanding of the inclusive education concept, but ignores context-specificity. By not accompanying their India programme with any disability-focused component, SCUK is in danger of allowing children with disabilities to remain the last priority—a fact acknowledged by the Delhi-based monitoring report team. Other international NGOs, such as Christoffel Blinden Mission, do not work for attitudinal change so much as on the financial support of local hospitals with eye units in remote rural areas, rehabilitation centres, special schools, and vocational centres for diverse disabilities run by local NGOs, many of which are Christian missionary-founded.

Private Schools

The explosive growth of private schools in recent years in India, in both urban and rural areas, is seen by many to be a result of dissatisfaction with the poor quality education provision in government schools. However, the private schools which have been voluntarily implementing inclusive education, are mostly found in urban areas, demonstrating the geographical inequalities so prevalent in the Indian context. In addition, as these private schools require the payment of fees, this inclusive education is not accessible to all, and so somewhat exclusive, although some admit 'bright' children from deprived backgrounds as a charitable gesture.

The adoption of inclusive education was found to be partly related to government pressure, partly to middle or upper class parental pressure for their own children with disabilities to be educated in the mainstream, and partly to the need for private schools to be seen as innovative in a highly competitive market. The educational status of parents played an important part in the direct academic support of their child, potentially allowing for inadequate teaching practices to go unaltered. There was little support for the teachers, with no formal training and a lack of communication and co-ordination with management or fellow teachers. Teacher motivation and an exam-oriented curriculum were seen as barriers to the adoption of IE, as were the attitudes of parents of other children in the school who did not accept that children with disabilities should be in the same class as their non-disabled child.

Education Policy

While there are policies in place to address the perceived educational needs of children with disabilities, there appear to be a number of issues that are leading to sporadic policy implementation, alongside several institutional and attitudinal constraints.

Administrative structure

Since 1976, education has been the joint responsibility of the Centre and States—the former gives policy frameworks and budgetary support, while the 32 diverse states (including Union Territories) organize, structure, and implement their own policies. While cultural variations add depth to this context, they can make it almost impossible for Central Government policies to reach everyone due to each state's individual interpretation of such policy.

Central Government admits that: "a major challenge in national planning is to reconcile the planning priorities of states with the national plan frame." This reflects the possibility of competing stakeholder objectives and cultural differences affecting the implementation of well-intentioned central policy such as inclusive education, a dilemma that affects many decentralized systems. The fact that, "cultural differences ... impact profoundly on service delivery systems that are transferred from one region to another," may absolve both Central and State administration of responsibility. The central government blames the State, while the state blames resource constraints or a lack of community interest, in an environment lacking any kind of accountability mechanism apart from the collection of data, which is easily manipulated. Hence, decentralization can also highlight weak capacity at local level and the need for development.

An additional bureaucratic tension, which is creating parallel systems, is the fact that children with disabilities in special schools come under the poorly performing Ministry of Social Justice and Empowerment (MSJE), while those in the mainstream come under the Department of Education in the Ministry of Human Resource Development (MHRD). This categorization is a further reflection of the cultural perception of children with disabilities in need of welfare rather than equality of opportunity. Although each department manages its own education programmes with inclusive education components, Singal finds evidence of concern that "children are dispersed across too many departments" with the result that the MHRD and MSJE "do not share a common ground" resulting in "duplication, divergent qualities and lack of uniformity". Despite apparent awareness of this issue, both ministries are currently named simultaneously as implementing agencies in the detailed framework for the 2006 MHRD Draft Action Plan for Inclusive Education.

Inclusive education policy

Recommendations to send children with disabilities to mainstream schools were first made in the Sargent Report in 1944, and again in 1964 by the Kothari

Commission. Despite this, change has been slow, with segregation in special schools dominating the scene until recently. Several education acts and promizes have been passed or mooted by Central Government in India in the past twenty years, although they do not seem to tackle the roots of attitudinal barriers to inclusion. For example, in 1993 the Delhi Declaration on Education for All promised to "...ensure a place for every child in a school or appropriate education programme according to his or her capabilities". This issue of 'capabilities' is key to the varied interpretations of 'inclusivity' of children, the focus on the child's abilities diverting attention away from inadequate teaching methods. This is perhaps true for some teachers, but the continued development of government and NGO teacher training programmes would also appear to show awareness of the need for pedagogical change.

The 1995 Persons with Disability Act (PDA) states that disabled children should be educated in integrated settings where possible, although it seems that the lack of implementation may be due to there being no enforcement agency for this legislation. In fact, section 71 of the PDA protects the government and local authorities from prosecution. Legislation and policy concerning IE must be evaluated in the context of progress toward implementation as well as the effectiveness of monitoring and evaluation. However, as inclusive education outcomes in developing contexts are such an undeveloped research area it is almost impossible to discover to what extent and how these legislative acts are implemented or not, and what kind of impact they may have at the grassroots level.

Despite the promotion of inclusive education, government documents focus on inclusive education as being about including children with disabilities in the *education system*, but not specifically the mainstream. This focus is seen by some as needed and fair because of the previous government focus on other disadvantaged groups, demonstrating how policy is focused on the majority as there are more girls or SC/ST children for example, than children with disabilities. However, inclusion in the education system is not the same as inclusion in the mainstream. If attending mainstream school is the 'norm', then being out of these schools can exacerbate difference and marginalize vulnerable children further.

Despite this, while different types of schooling being deemed appropriate for different strata of society can be perceived as fundamentally exclusionary, some parents may prefer their child to attend an alternative education institution, perhaps to gain a vocational skill, to gain the benefits of medical rehabilitation, or simply to avoid bullying. Itinerant teachers, community based rehabilitation, special schools, non-formal education, and vocational centres all have something to offer children marginalized by the mainstream in educational terms such as acquiring literacy, living skills and financial independence. In addition, an alternative education institution may not necessarily be sub-standard, perhaps even offering higher quality teaching and learning processes than a local government school.

It is arguable that special education is in fact regarded as superior in India due to its 'preferred' status, and that it is inclusion in the mainstream that is currently seen as the resource-constrained inferior alternative. However, the limited coverage of mainly urban-based, impairment-specific special schools in India may result in the exclusion of children with disabilities who do not 'fit' the categorization of these institutions or who live in rural areas. Inclusive education may be the only way of facilitating educational access for these children.

A focus on physical access to school, rather than access to curriculum and equal treatment once in the classroom, is an additional barrier to inclusion, possibly resulting in drop out.

While physical infrastructure and enrolment are important, they are seemingly simple access issues to address, and easy to demonstrate progress in through quantitative data. It is the more complicated constraints of what happens in the classroom and in the community at large, fundamentally guided by attitudes towards children with disabilities, that are the most difficult to change. However, they are equally essential in ensuring access, whether in terms of enrolment or academic participation. Hence, negative attitudes can be seen perhaps as the most inhibitive constraint of them all.

Government policy focus on resources and physical access, or infrastructure such as ramps in schools, and the notion of social justice through the equal distribution of benefit, seems to be more about inputs, not processes like pedagogy, curriculum or attitudes. It is this focus which results in selection of the relatively few "easy-to-accommodate children" with mild or moderate disabilities that do not need too much specialist assistance. However, this could be understood as a pragmatic approach in a context with inadequate infrastructure and few specialist teachers available to assist inclusion mainstream classrooms. This apparently selective inclusion, with children being 'prepared' in order to be 'ready' for the mainstream seems to give inclusive education in India an exclusive flavour, although this may be because homogeneity in the classroom can be perceived as an essential prerequisite to enable good teaching. This appears to directly contradict northern understandings of inclusive education being, by definition, all about embracing diversity in the classroom.

Despite islands of government programme success, disability budgets remain under-used, and reserved jobs unfilled. These are sure signs of the sporadic implementation of inclusive education, as is the persistently low percentage of children with disabilities being in school. This is a result of the complex interaction of issues and constraints that vary in influence from state to state, let alone from classroom to classroom.

In addition, not only are most special schools found in urban centres, but also awareness of the development of inclusive education is limited to cities when the majority of disabled learners live in rural areas. This rural/urban disparity does not just affect children with disabilities but other marginalized groups too, as schools in the more remote, or poorer areas tend to lack both human and physical resources, highlighting the need for a reconceptualization of inclusive education policy as a whole school issue.

Teacher education

Many academics in the field of inclusive education point to teacher education and school leadership as essential for the implementation of inclusive education in the classroom, yet the standard of teacher training courses across India varies hugely, and they usually approach the inclusion of children with disabilities from a deficit perspective. In the general teacher education diplomas and degrees available nationwide, there is an optional 'special needs' paper to train and 'prepare' teachers to identify and diagnose disability. However, it is not an integral part of the training, and it does not train teachers to deal with diversity or challenge negative attitudes. This reinforces the 'difference' of children with disabilities who, some believe, can only be taught by teachers qualified specifically for them. However, it is ultimately teacher treatment of students in the classroom, rather than the training per say, that would reinforce this difference.

Interestingly, distrust in both the special and mainstream education systems leads some parents to keep their children with disabilities at home for fear of their abuse or neglect in the classroom, which may then be interpreted by teachers as a lack of community interest in education for their children. This raises the question of how teachers are being trained to include children with disabilities and to what extent they put this training into daily practice. Without access to qualitative research data specifically observing these teacher education outcomes, it is impossible to know. While it may be true that a lack of teacher training to deal with diversity or challenge negative attitudes results in a specialist, medical deficit, focus, there is certainly a need to train teachers in specific disabilities for students who could benefit from special lessons in skills such as Braille, sign-language or speech therapy.

There is evidence to suggest that many teachers do not feel equipped to teach children with disabilities and complain that they need more time to instruct these students. Many government programmes have included a teacher training component in an attempt to instigate institutional change. However, a 'special needs' focus and a lack of training for management, combined with didactic training methodology do little to alter the classroom status quo, especially when responsibility is shifted onto a specialist resource teacher rather than methods altered to suit all students. When teacher training is taken out of the context of programme islands and geographically accessible environments, teachers are found to be reluctant to attend training because it takes place in their free time and holidays. Teacher posts remain unfilled, even in Delhi, because of a lack of qualified personnel, which can also lead to state employment of under-qualified teachers, further impacting on school quality. However, a teacher can be fully qualified, but if the training is sub-standard it will still have a negative impact on teaching and learning quality in the classroom, whereas an under-qualified, poorly paid teacher with some imagination and innovative practices may have a positive effect.

The poor quality educational provision in many schools is reflected in the fact that many government job reservations for adults with disabilities remain unfilled. Some may interpret this as due to the lack of ability many in Indian society believe is inherent in the disabled community. It is more likely to be directly related to the fact that so few children with disabilities get to, or stay in, school, that there is a lack of qualified, let alone confident, candidates. However, although school (and pedagogical) quality would appear to be one of the keys to an end to marginalization for children with disabilities, the current locational inclusion focus of inclusive education in India is a major obstacle to the unlocking of this doorway to freedom and empowerment.

Resources

While the 1995 Persons with Disabilities Act perhaps moved the education of children with disabilities into the main frame its focus on disability as a resource, not social, issue, can be seen as a wasted opportunity to tackle societal barriers. The rationale behind inclusive education as an economic necessity rather than ideological preference, cannot be ignored in a resource-constrained context. Inclusive education is an alternative for developed education systems but it is an inevitability for developing systems.

A small pool of resources combined with high demand, suggests that the development of the mainstream would be a more financially effective and efficient way to go. This could result in smaller classes and better teaching which would benefit all students. Arguably, resources would not be so limited after all if all specialist institution funding was moved to the mainstream, which may explain why Thomas argues that there are indeed sufficient resources in India to implement inclusive education. However, this solution could mean that the essential services which some special schools provide would be spread wider, and thinner. Indeed, the government could find that the cost of well-resourced specialist provision spread across all schools rather than centralized in resource centres more financially prohibitive than the current situation.

Although external donor support can be perceived as insignificant in the context of the Central government's overall education budget, there appears to be extensive external funding of programmes aiming to improve accessibility of mainstream schools to marginalized children, including those with disabilities. While external assistance can help the government to tackle its resource 'crunch' in the short-term, it may also be having a negative effect on the political will needed to make a 6 per cent GDP allocation to education. This lack of political will is further reflected in the seemingly continuous string of externally-assisted government education programmes that fall short of their goals. With no consequences of an accountability mechanism in sight, they are simply left to wither and die while everyone moves on to the next programme with its glittering tranche of all-new funding and revised goals.

After the *Shiksha Yatra* march of over 50,000 people in 2001, the 86th amendment to the Constitution finally made elementary education for all children a Fundamental Right in 2002. Despite the impressive impact this rights-based campaign appears to have had on pushing through this long-discussed amendment, it remains to be seen to what extent this right will be fulfilled and how it will be interpreted in the long term. It seems that the government has already cited financial constraints in its failed implementation of the amendment.

IMPLICATIONS

While there is no shortage of issues and constraints in the interpretation and implementation of inclusive education in India, it is important to remember that it is at a very early stage of conceptualization and implementation. The fact that it is being discussed and in some places implemented, albeit falteringly, demonstrates a willingness to engage with elements of a new concept that has the potential to be developed in the future in a positive manner. This section will explore the implications that these issues have for possible areas of development that could move forward mutual understandings of how inclusive education could benefit the Indian education system, or rather the people in it.

Policy Implementation

So long as the struggle to achieve compulsory education for a majority of children takes precedence over meeting the needs of those with disabilities, change for children with disabilities will continue to be sporadic and painfully slow. The division of educational responsibility for children, between the MSJE for those with disabilities and the MHRD for those without, can only exacerbate this struggle, and highlight the 'different' nature of children with disabilities' needs and the special needs focus of inclusive education with it. This implies that if inclusive education came under one ministry alone, most probably the MHRD, potentially both conceptualization and implementation could be clarified and promoted, while the needs of children with disabilities could finally be mainstreamed.

The absence of accountability mechanisms, which results in poor policy implementation, suggests that in order to ensure implementation of 1995's rhetorically positive Persons with Disabilities Act, some kind of legal enforcement mechanism needs to be created, perhaps related to resource allocation or government employee contract renewal. In turn, enforcement needs a disciplined inspection network of regular monitoring and evaluation by external evaluators in order to ascertain whether policy is indeed being implemented, and to what standard. However, the manipulation of data, as seen in Operation Blackboard, is, "undermining a vital tool of school management and planning". Unless the accuracy of data is rewarded, as opposed to the inflation of enrolment figures or achievement levels, this manipulation will continue. The absence of reliable assessment and strong enforcement mechanisms is perhaps one of the reasons why so many government programmes whither away, targets unfulfilled, and government departments remain unchanged despite repeated failure.

The size and diversity of India dictates the necessity for state governments to take the responsibility of implementing central policy. Not only does a lack of accountability contribute to the diversity of state performance in inclusive education, as with all policy, but also variations in local government administrative capacity can have a disparity-inducing effect. Training of government officials of all levels for managing monitoring and evaluation systems or enforcing accountability are just as important as training in conceptual awareness of inclusive education and disability issues. Management reform at the local level is essential for sustainability and long-term change, but in this context it depends on the political will of each state to instigate reform. However, without the inclusion, understanding and good will of the administrators holding the purse-strings at local government level, state policy will not be implemented either.

School Quality

As disabling educational environments affect all children, not only those who are identified as having impairments, it is essential that school quality issues are identified and addressed. The re-conceptualization of inclusive education as a school quality issue could have significant impact on educational change in India for all children. With the reconceptualization of inclusive education, from students with special needs to all children, school quality could improve nationwide.

Teacher education is certainly key to this metamorphosis, but without a wider understanding of the meaning of IE for all learners, it will make little difference. This has been proved to date with the huge investment into government teacher training programmes that have yielded little long-term fruit in the shape of pedagogical revolution. The non-implementation of child-centred teaching methods may be influenced by a focus on theory rather than practice, the brevity of teacher training courses without follow-up or feedback, or simply a lack of basic teacher knowledge leading to insecurity that they will not be able to answer a question. Nevertheless, this failure to change pedagogy is not only due to teacher education course design, but also the reality of 24.5 per cent teacher absenteeism, combined with resource-constrained institutions with large classes and an inflexible curriculum which force the teachers to return to didactic habits in order to cope.

The class size need not be a hindrance in the practice of child-centred pedagogy if training takes into account the context-specific knowledge and methods teachers already use in their large, diverse classes, and progresses from this point. A further hindrance to new pedagogy is that parental expectations are of exam results, not of 'joyful learning'. Hence, the pressure on teachers is even greater to avoid change. This exam 'backwash' no doubt contributes to the notion of within-child deficit and faith in IQ which can only be altered by attitudinal change aided by teacher education. For example, exam success from the practice of innovative teaching methodology, as demonstrated in the SIDH programme, can change attitudes towards child-centred pedagogy.

It is not only teachers who benefit from training, but local government administrators too, as their support and understanding of inclusive education could provide invaluable assistance to institutional innovation. This reflects the belief that good working relationships are critical to the implementation of inclusive education. SCUK recommends a whole school approach to the inclusion of children with disabilities, in that all teachers are consulted and trained, not a select few 'specialists'. In addition, it is essential that teachers are supported not only by strong educational management with a clear strategy to improve school quality, but also by parents and the local community. Ideally, all stakeholders should participate in the inclusive education process including the child.

The apparent exclusivity of selective inclusion of children with disabilities in the mainstream, encouraged perhaps by the 'specialist' nature of teacher training for children with special educational needs, may seem alien to northern spectators living within societies with a stronger consciousness of disability as a social issue. However, while Singal criticizes government pragmatism in avoiding deeper inclusion issues by focusing on physical and sensory disabilities only as suitable for mainstream education, it is worth considering that with such a mountain to climb it may be better to start somewhere and then progress. Perhaps deeper reflection will come after the successful inclusion of a few.

Attitudinal Change

Many of the issues and constraints surrounding the interpretation and implementation of inclusive education encountered in the Indian context, are not unique to India. However, the all-pervasive caste system, as a barrier to attitudinal change, is. The context-specificity of this socio-religious construct is a factor that cannot be ignored when looking at the implications for the future of any aspect of life in India. However, the caste system will not disappear overnight, but it is a highly constructed world within which all implications must be considered and all potential change would take place. In a more positive light, it may be that by being a fifth caste, or even outside the system, works to the advantage of people with disabilities in that their development could be perceived as being unrelated to caste, and so more amenable to innovative thinking.

While attitudes which are deep-rooted in cultural assumptions are probably the most difficult aspect of change, they have influence across the board, ranging from community, to school, to government. This suggests that attitudinal change should be considered an integral part of any inclusive education programme or plan, ranging from DPOs raising awareness at grassroots level, to teacher education, to administrative capacity-building, to policy-making. Self-criticism and analysis is an important part of the attitudinal change process however, and could be very difficult to instigate in many stakeholders, depending on their personality. Hence, this element of change would undoubtedly need the ability for stakeholders to be prepared for conflict, and potential chaos.

As attitudes are based on beliefs, they can be changed when presented with new information such as inclusion success stories of children with disabilities. Islands of change may have limited coverage, but they can be scaled-up and lead to broader change with advocacy. For example, village teachers in SIDH primary schools found that once they had achieved exam success by using some Montessori-inspired teaching methods, they gained credibility and were then able to experiment with more innovative pedagogy. However, as a micro-level NGO programme, the NGO-trained village 'instructors' were perhaps able to be more flexible in their approach to curriculum than formally-trained teachers in a government school. Community-based rehabilitation has also been found to assist in attitudinal change.

Currently hindered by personal rivalries and competition for resources, Indian DPOs are failing the people they are intending to assist through their lack of co-ordination with each other. DPOs such as Action on Disability and Development (ADD), which is working on building up grassroots civil society networks, and Able Disabled All People Together (ADAPT), which is a Mumbai-based advocacy group for attitudinal and policy change, are good examples of groups that approach disability issues from their attitudinal foundations. However, the majority of DPOs in India do not effectively represent the interests of disabled people or hold up the state to public scrutiny, being urban-focused and top-down in their approach. The absence of a single cross-disability voice in India as a result of inter-organizational rivalry and the movement being divided between impairments, has resulted in many being unaware of their rights as a disabled person, and DPOs lobbying for issues that are largely peripheral to the needs and lives of the majority of India's disabled population, who are poor and live in rural areas.

Action on Disability and Development (ADD), and DPOs doing similar work with grassroots advocacy, could play a key role in unifying the voice of adults and children with disabilities in order to apply political pressure and raise awareness amongst other people with disabilities of their entitlements and rights. For example, although a Gandhian long march may not be practical for those with impaired mobility, DPOs across India could unite to modify a form of march to empower people with disabilities and disseminate information. DPOs, if unified, have the potential to initiate conceptual clarity of inclusive education with a bottom-up approach, opening up debate nationwide. In addition, as a large, well-funded organization that promotes the voice of the child, if they included a disability-focused component in their India strategy, SCUK could make a significant difference to advocacy for children with disabilities and their right to mainstream education.

Research

While there is a noticeable lack of in-depth empirical and academic research on inclusive education in India, this can also be seen as reflecting the preliminary stage such discussions are at in this context and the room for development of a constructive discourse with further research.

This absence of information suggests that there is a dire need for more research into both the implementation and impact of inclusive education in India. There are large gaps in the hard-to-access research, both qualitative and quantitative, on IE in India. The apparent desire for change hinted at by the slowly developing discussion around inclusive education at all levels, can only be fulfilled if it is planned for. In order to constructively implement inclusive education for all children, planning must not only be adapted according to context, but also include funding for continual research, monitoring and impact evaluation from all stakeholders' perspectives. This includes the children's voices, and especially from those with disabilities. The long-term filling of the current research gap in IE in India could make a significant contribution to a sustainable, adaptable process of change. Diagnosis of implementation and quality monitoring reports could lead to valuable lessons learned. Both quantitative research to assess the extent of provision and need, and qualitative research to assess the impact of current provision, could provide an invaluable contribution to a continually evolving monitoring, evaluation and planning network.

The invisibilization of people with disabilities is reflected in the lack of valid and reliable data bemoaned by academics, who suggest that the only way for international and local assistance to move forward for people with disabilities is to collect specific disability-focused data to enable project planning. However, a household survey or national census, both of which are often answered only by the head of the household or by proxy, may present inaccurate data if family members with disabilities are hidden by their relatives who may be ashamed of them. In addition, only obvious impairments may be counted as disabilities, excluding mental and learning disabilities, and so resulting in "selective reporting".

Not only do multiple definitions and understandings of 'disability' make this data collection problematic, but also, survey and costs can be prohibitive and present ethical concerns when carried out without being followed up by a service for those surveyed. Without the data, children with disabilities may continue to be 'invisiblized', but it is difficult to pinpoint exactly how extensive, or expensive, data collection needs to be before a service can be provided. Perhaps the initial count from within the framework of the 2001 National Census will assist in the provision of basic education services, segregated or inclusive. This may then raise awareness and so reveal further demand as parents approach institutions with the desire for their children with disabilities to be educated too. The next stage would be to disaggregate survey data, especially at household and school level, to enable policy makers to explore the links between different forms of social exclusion, and how disability is a part of the experience of all groups (e.g. caste/disability, or gender/disability) with basic education access issues. Certainly, there is little research to date on the social background of children with disabilities. This would highlight the importance for all education programmes to include a disability component.

From a qualitative perspective, there currently appears to be very little research assessing the impact of teaching and learning processes in the classroom post-teacher education, specifically aimed at inclusive education. Similarly, research recording the beliefs, experiences, and desires for the future of all stakeholders involved (such as education officials, administrators, teachers, parents), including the often neglected child's voice, is hard to find, and could assist in furthering understandings of the current situation and how it can be improved. Action research, monitoring and evaluation, and impact assessments could all assist in the improved planning and implementation of IE programmes for the local government officials and school management who administer the policy, and teaching staff who are the key to educational access within the classroom. Without research on inclusive education outcomes, lessons-learned cannot be applied to make implementation more effective, and so schools more accessible to all learners.

3

EDUCATION OF CHILDREN WITH AUTISM

WHAT IS AUTISM?

The term 'autism' is used in here to mean 'autistic spectrum disorders' as a whole. It covers a number of different diagnostic categories in medical terms, and describes what is considered to be common to all of those diagnoses. The aim is to arrive at an educational definition of autism from which, in part, a child's special educational needs may be derived. Autism is defined and diagnosed medically from its characteristic pattern of behaviours, yet there are no behaviours that of themselves will unequivocally indicate autism. Concentration on the behaviour alone will often lead to misleading interpretations and thus to inappropriate treatment. Behaviour is essential in our recognition of autism but, by itself, it does not help us understand the condition or decide how to approach it.

Autism was first described by Kanner in 1943. He originally believed that all children with autism had normal levels of intellectual functioning but this has been shown to be incorrect. There is a substantial group of children with autism who have additional general learning difficulties. Autism also commonly co-occurs with a language disorder, and may co-occur with a motor or sensory impairment. At almost the same time, Asperger was also identifying a group of children as having autism.

Kanner's work became well known and had great influence throughout the world, but it is only comparatively recently that Asperger's work has been taken up internationally. Diagnostic systems now use Asperger's syndrome to refer to people with autism who have normal levels of general intellectual functioning and good structural language skills. It is not clear whether this is separate from Kanner's autism or whether it represents autism without additional language or intellectual impairment. However, for the purposes of education, the same understandings and teaching approaches will benefit all children with autis- tic spectrum disorders of whatever kind.

Wing has identified a triad of impairments which now underpin all diagnostic criteria for autistic spectrum disorders. It is this triad that expresses what is common to the disorders within the spectrum. The triad expresses difficulties in three areas of development as indicative of autism and no one area can be taken on its own to be 'autistic'. It is the triad in full that indicates that the child may be following a different developmental path, and, if there is only one area of impairment, then that may arise from an entirely different cause.

When we are considering the special educational needs of individuals, we need to consider all those who will have specific needs arising from their autistic spectrum disorder, in relation to the curriculum offered, the teaching approach and the environment. Within this group there will be those who have additional profound and multiple learning difficulties through to those within the normal range of intelligence. The range of difficulties in the triad of impairments are:

— *Social impairment:* There are difficulties in interacting with both adults and peers. This will include the classically 'aloof' child, but will also include those who respond to social interaction, although they may be unable to initiate it, through to the 'active but odd' child who seeks social interaction but is socially naive and cannot quite 'get it right'.

— *Communication impairment:* There are difficulties in all aspects of communication. The autistic problem concerns communication rather than language per se. One child may have good grammar and articulation and may speak fluently, but his or her speech may have odd intonation, may show echolalia (repeating) and 'reversal' of pronouns (at least when young) and understanding of speech may be literal. There will be difficulties in holding conversations, with the child with autism talking 'at' rather than 'to' or 'with' people. There will also be difficulties in understanding and using facial expressions, body postures and communicative gestures. Another child may have the same difficulties in understanding all forms of communication, but will have no speech and will not easily compensate with sign or communicative gesture. Communication, at all levels of ability, is directed at getting needs met, rather than sharing information or interests.

— *Flexibility impairment:* There are difficulties in flexible thinking and behaviour. This is shown in repetitive stereotyped behaviour and, in some individuals, an extreme reaction to change in expected situations or routines. Play tends not to be creative or truly symbolic (although symbolic play acts may be copied) and is often isolated. It may involve spinning objects or a fascination with light or angles. The more able show similar difficulties, but in a more intellectually demanding way, in their development of obsessive interests or 'hobbies', that are pursued at the expense of everything else. Understanding of fiction is minimal, or related to stock characters. Learning is easiest by rote and is difficult to generalize.

Of course, the same fundamental disability will have different effects in different individuals and even in the same individual over time. So, while some individuals with autism avoid social contact, like Kanner's cases, others are merely passive, or even actively seek social contact but are unable to understand it fully or get it right in practice. The special needs of any individual will, of course, not be determined solely by developmental difficulties but will be the result of interactions between abilities and disabilities and the learning environment. As the child grows to adulthood, the effect of education and the kind of experiences the person has had will have an increasing role in determining current behaviour and ways of thinking.

As indicated above, there is no one behaviour that is 'autistic' and it is the total pattern of behaviour, plus the reasons that underlie it, that indicates autism. That is one of the reasons why professionals cannot just operate at this behavioural level. Thus, a congenitally blind child may share some of the characteristics seen in autism, without necessarily having autism, and a child who has been severely traumatized may also appear to show the same 'features'. The behaviours produced may be very similar, but they have a different cause and, therefore, a different prognosis. The blind child will learn other ways of knowing the world and the 'autistic' behaviour will lessen over time. Similarly, the traumatized or abused child, once placed in a secure caring environment, will learn to trust again and the 'autistic' behaviour will go.

Children with autism will also improve, given the right treatment, but they follow a different developmental path, due to differences at the biological level, and so the treatment and education they need will also be different. It should also be remembered that many apparently 'autistic' behaviours can be seen in anyone under a sufficient degree of stress and this suggests that what may appear as an 'autistic feature' may in fact be a secondary effect of stress.

None of the claims for a complete 'cure' or recovery from autism have been completely validated by independent researchers. There are also anecdotal reports of young infants who appear at eighteen months or so to have the symptoms of autism, but then to 'grow out of it'; this is particularly likely where the child has been premature or suffers from a sensory loss. All we can say for certain is that autism is a life-long condition but that there may, of course, be considerable improvement over time, especially with appropriate education. It is also true that some more able individuals do learn to function in ways that may be indistinguishable from the norm. It is a moot point whether they can then be said to be 'cured' of their autism.

IDENTIFYING SPECIAL NEEDS IN AUTISM

An understanding of the fundamental difficulties faced by a child is crucial to developing a curriculum and a teaching approach that addresses that child's needs. Responding at the level of behaviour only, may lead to unhelpful or even damaging misinterpretations of the child's behaviour and a consequent failure to identify the true educational needs. Each child will still be an individual and will need careful observation to determine his/her level of understanding and capacity, but that observation needs to be informed by the knowledge of what particular difficulties the child is facing in making sense of the world.

An example of this in practice is the case of a young girl with autism who came to a specialist school at the age of seven years. She had good structural language skills and could speak in sentences. She also had reasonably well-developed self-help skills, having been toilet trained from the age of two years. However, once she started school, a problem had emerged with respect to her toileting. Whenever she knew where the toilet was she took herself there, without difficulty, but, if she did not know where the toilet was, she wet and soiled herself.

This was a puzzle to her teachers because she appeared to have all the prerequisite skills to ask to go to the toilet and yet the problem persisted. By the time she entered the specialist setting she had undergone a series of different interventions aimed at resolving this 'problem' but all to no avail. Her mother, in desperate frustration, had punished her for soiling by hitting her with a hairbrush; the home where she went for respite care had given her cold showers for the same reason; family therapy sessions had focused on resolving supposed tensions at home and had discussed marital problems with the parents and interpreted her behaviour as a symbolic 'giving' of herself in terms of her faeces to test their love for her; a visiting clinical psychologist had put her on a behavioural programme whereby she could earn 'points' for being clean and dry and she could save these for horse-riding sessions, which she loved.

None of these 'interventions' had any effect. They failed because they were related to different interpretations of her behaviour and how it could be controlled but none of them took account of her autism. What was needed was the understanding that, although she appeared to have all the skills to express her needs she lacked one vital element: she did not understand about the need to communicate. Once this was recognized, a solution could be worked on. Her teachers blocked her taking herself to the toilet, in situations where she knew where it was, and prompted her to ask for the toilet. Once this had been done consistently for a few days, she changed from taking herself to the toilet to asking for it. In new situations, her new habit of asking meant the problem was solved. Once she reached her teens another problem arose in that asking just anyone would not be appropriate and might put her at risk of abuse. She was then trained to recognize that she did not know where the toilet was and to develop a range of strategies to find out. Thus, it is important to take account of the diagnosis when interpreting the behaviour of the child and when working out teaching approaches. Education remains the one treatment approach with the best 'track record' for dealing with the difficulties associated with autism. It is not just a matter of 'access' to education as a statutory right for children with autism, but about how education can have a central role in 'remediating' the effects of autism (not 'curing' it) and improving the quality of life for individuals with autism throughout their life span.

Primary and Secondary Difficulties

The problem with any developmental disorder like autism is that an initial difficulty can lead to restrictions in the child's learning opportunities which then go on to cause further secondary difficulties. One of the key roles of education is to identify key developmental areas that have been missed or distorted and to build up strategies and experiences to compensate for the lost opportunities. Where possible, education may even get in early enough to prevent the secondary difficulties from occurring at all.

Yet it must be remembered that autism is a biological difficulty, so it is of little use merely to put the child through the stages of early development again; if he or she were capable of learning from that experience they would have done so in the first place. What education must seek to do is to find ways of achieving the same ends through routes to which the child with autism has access.

Such routes involve a slowing down of interaction to give more opportunities for the child to process the information presented and to formulate a response. They involve using short sentences or phrases with greater pauses between them, for the same reason, and making everything as explicit as possible. This does not mean that everything has to be explained in words, but actions may need to be exaggerated to get the child's attention, games may need to be played alongside rather than facing the child and facing a mirror so both their own and the other's face can be seen at the same time, and the tuning of the interaction may need to be emphasized through music or singing.

But the most important aspect of working effectively with children with autism is understanding them. It will not be enough just to respond to behaviours, but rather to have some understanding of the more fundamental underlying difficulties that offer a rationale for those behaviours.

Failure in Inter-relatedness

If there is a fundamental difficulty in recognizing and responding to emotional and social cues, the individual with autism will have particular difficulty with those that do not result in clearly differentiated facial expressions. They may learn to identify 'happy' with a smiling face, for example, but then will never understand what a 'brave smile' is; they may learn to label a sad face as such but still have no idea of the underlying emotion and so are still capable at laughing when they see the funny expression of sadness on their mother's face and water coming from their mother's eyes. This lack of empathy can be hurtful and can lead to others judging them as cruel or cold. They are also likely to show poor emotional expression themselves.

Yet there is no evidence that people with autism experience emotions any less than others. In fact, their behaviour suggests that their feelings are often very strong and that they often have great difficulty in controlling them. The problem lies in not being aware of their emotions at an explicit level, which also makes it more difficult for them to exert control. It may also mean that their expression of emotions may be primitive and in the form of emotional outbursts.

The teacher who understands these difficulties may still need to develop short-term strategies for overcoming reluctance to sit with others and to get the pupil to a situation where she/he is able to learn in a group, but she/he will also be working on long-term approaches to build up understanding of emotions. This may be by making them explicit, by teaching about the perceptual indicators of emotion and how these vary together to express emotion—facial expression, voice quality, body posture, actions etc. so that people are no longer so unpredictable and frightening.

Awareness of emotions will also have greater benefits in learning on a more general plane and making that learning more flexible since this is one of the key roles that emotions play in cognition. Such understandings of autism also indicate the value of approaches that foster emotional sharing through the use of music to accompany social actions or through joining the children in their own area of intense interest.

Failure to Establish an Experiencing Self

Thinking and learning in autism may be very different from the norm. Individuals with autism may have difficulty in establishing a sense of themselves at an experiential level and this lack of an experiencing self would have a number of direct consequences on development and behaviour.

There will be problems in developing a sense of agency. This will lead in turn to difficulties in using the first person pronoun 'I', in an inability to be aware of intentions and therefore to plan actions, in a lack of goal-directedness in actions, and thus in difficulty with spontaneous or creative behaviour.

If one does not have an experiencing self then there is no sense of events happening to oneself; rather, they just happen. The individual may have a concept of him/herself but it is limited to autobiographical knowledge, knowing oneself from the 'outside' as it were. An experiencing self is also important in memory processing and so a failure to develop this will lead to poor personal episodic memory. This will mean that all episodic memories have to be cued in some way i.e. there will be no way of searching the memory. It also means that self-expression will be limited to what others have 'fed in'.

Without a sense of oneself in one's dealings with the world, there will be a failure to adopt an 'attitudinal stance'. This will lead to difficulties in 'foregrounding' relevant information, and difficulties in categorization. This may in extreme cases lead to failures to discriminate.

Without an understanding of these kinds of difficulties a teacher is at a loss in attempting to improve thinking and learning and has to resort to teaching that builds on habits that are cued in an increasing range of situations, in the hope of producing generalisable learning. Understanding the source of the difficulty may mean that these compensatory strategies are used for much of the time but it also enables the teacher to focus attention on more effective strategies at the cognitive level.

For example, at a purely behavioural level it seems either incomprehensible, or a matter of motivation, that the child may appear to have such an excellent memory in some contexts and not in others. Knowing that the child may not be experiencing things in the same way helps the teacher realize that memories will need to be cued and she/he can then teach the child to pay attention to certain cues and how to use those to trigger the memory when necessary. Children with autism may also find it easier to say what happened to a classmate on a trip than to tell what they have experienced themselves. The teacher can also decide to devote some time to the 'remedial' task of helping the child establish this sense of an experiencing self through the use of reflection in the way suggested by Powell and Jordan.

Executive Function Deficit

An executive function involves processes such as planning, monitoring and directing activities, reflecting on one's mental states, and achieving a goal by flexible means. Certainly, it is true that all of these functions are disturbed in autism although children with learning difficulties without autism may share at least some of these problems.

One particular consequence would be difficulty in modifying behaviour in relation to feedback. Thus, the child with autism persists in actions even though they are clearly seen to 'fail' or are punished in some way. This is just the kind of behaviour that is often attributed to willful disobedience, failure to attend or simple provocation. Once it is understood that the child's actions are simply triggered by the situation, then teachers should feel less frustrated and more able to plan to help the child overcome this difficulty.

Understanding this difficulty enables one to see the futility of aversive measures intended to punish behaviour or of nagging or cajoling the child. There will be only two ways of getting the child to change his or her behaviour. The first, and usually the best, way is to alter the situation so that a particular behaviour is no longer triggered.

For example, a six year old boy had developed a 'habit' of tearing his bedclothes every night. Scolding him, even hitting him, had no effect. A warm air heater was placed in his bedroom and all his bed linen was removed.

Now there was nothing to tear and nothing to trigger that particular behaviour, but to ensure success it was also necessary to alter the child's own state. A vigorous rough and tumble game with his father was introduced for half an hour before bedtime, followed by a warm bath. He was also given a toy to fiddle with in bed, and gentle music was played through a tape recorder. Bedtime was made an hour later than formerly. Almost immediately, the period of restless behaviour in bed prior to sleep ceased. After a few weeks, the boy had developed the new habit of going to bed to sleep. At that stage, the heating was reduced and gradually bed linen was reintroduced. The behaviour remained under control.

The second approach, to changing behaviour is to prevent the child from performing the undesired behaviour in that situation and to train an alternative to take its place. This is the method of choice when the situation cannot be changed. This was the method used to prevent a little girl from sticking her hands in the steam from a boiling kettle. The priority was to find something she could do that would be satisfying for her but would not put her in danger nor too near the temptation of the steam. She enjoyed other activities involving perceptual distortions such as the steam provided, and, notably, she enjoyed blowing soap bubbles and popping them.

An intense programme was started whereby, whenever she saw a kettle begin to steam she was kept at a safe distance but physically guided to clap her hands loudly. At this signal, staff would present her with a bowl of soapy water and she was instructed on using it to blow bubbles. In a short while she began using the steam as a signal that she could 'ask' for the bubbles. She began to ask for the bubbles by clapping when there was no steam and this was allowed to a limited extent. After several months her habit of putting her hands in the steam had gone so that she was no longer prompted to ask for the bubbles if she did not do so spontaneously. Even so, adults had to remain vigilant lest the habit reappear.

DEVELOPING SOCIAL SKILLS OF CHILDREN WITH AUTISM

There is a difficulty in teaching social skills when the child with autism has little or no social understanding. What we call 'social behaviour' consists of the ability to share pleasure in the company of others and to respond to and initiate social behaviour in contexts that are, by their very nature, continually changing. Children with autism will experience difficulties in all these aspects and this will lead to further problems in teaching and learning.

Since education usually takes place in a social context, there will be management problems affecting pupils' access to all aspects of the curriculum. Direct teaching of social skills will also be required since there will be many aspects of social development that will not occur spontaneously and many compensatory strategies that will be needed. There is the further practical difficulty that teaching a social behaviour appropriate to a child at some point in her/his life may take so long that by the time it is achieved it is no longer appropriate.

Social Problems

It can be misleading to think that children with autism will necessarily be withdrawn. There is a wide continuum of social behaviour that is associated with autism, and the classic passive, solitary, and withdrawn child is only typical of one kind of child with autism, and not necessarily throughout the development even of that child. The preschool child who starts off very withdrawn may become more passive and tolerant of others in his or her middle school years and by the time adolescence is reached may have become very interested in social contact but may just not know how to get on with others and make friends.

Higher functioning children with autism do not necessarily start off being any less socially disabled than those with additional severe learning difficulties, although, clearly, the range of social behaviours they exhibit will be greater. As they grow older, however, the more able do generally become less socially disabled although in the population without autism there is no correlation between general intellectual level and social ability. Autism seems to be a special case in that respect in that those who do learn social interactions, appear to do so by different methods to those employed by normally developing children.

Attention getting strategies

Children with autism rarely attempt to share toys or

direct an adult's attention by pointing or looking at objects. They may be physically aware of the presence of an adult but seem unable to share a focus of visual attention. They appear to understand the use of the other person as an 'agent', but fail to show any appreciation that the other person has a perspective that can be shared or directed. They are able to take note of another's visual perspective, but this does not occur spontaneously and they cannot take the conceptual perspective of another. They do not understand about communication and so they may not realize that what they say or sign has to be directed to someone. Children with autism who speak may be found muttering to themselves or delivering messages to empty rooms. Children who sign may do so under the table, not realising that their 'communication' needs to be seen to be understood.

Children with autism, then, need to be taught to recognize attempts to gain their attention, to share the attention of others and to obtain and direct it where appropriate. It will be easier for the teacher or career to join in with the child's focus of attention at first, rather than expect the child to join the attention of the adult. Just as a mother might with a young baby, the teacher needs to comment on the activity the child is engaged on, or, especially for the non-verbal child, to join in that activity. If the child is making a pot from clay, for example, the teacher might also make his or her own pot, sitting alongside the child, instead of merely directing the child with instructions. This makes it easier to gain the child's attention in a relevant way and has the added advantage of providing an ongoing model of what the child is to do without continually prompting or nagging the child to keep on task. The children will need to be taught directly that there always needs to be someone to receive their communications; spoken or signed communications will need someone to hear or see them and that someone will need to have his or her attention captured before the children start to communicate. Speaking children can be taught to use vocatives or the person's name before they begin to speak. Non-speaking children may need to be taught specific ways of gaining attention according to the social context.

Physical withdrawal

It is sometimes difficult to tell if children with autism are actively withdrawing from people or whether it appears that way because they do not know how to relate to others and they are engaged in self-absorbing stereotyped activities. Nor is it clear whether such stereotypes are engaged in for their own sakes or as a way of shutting oneself off from others. Certainly, it has been found that children's responsiveness to their environment increases if their ritualistic behaviours are reduced.

Teachers should also remember that children with autism are just as likely to become depressed so that if a child in adolescence goes through a prolonged period of withdrawal when previously he or she had been much more sociable, treatment should be sought for the depression, just as one would for any child. Not all symptoms of disturbed behaviour should be put down to the autism.

Many approaches for working with children with autism do not let the child withdraw but insist on joining in with his or her chosen activity, albeit in a loving and accepting way. Some teachers take charge of the situation and also do not let the child withdraw, a method described as 'intrusive teaching'. Such methods form the basis of structured and directed approaches. There may be initial resistance on the part of the child to such contact but, if done regularly and consistently, it is usually accepted by the child who might even come in time to seek such regular contact from an adult.

Contact with peers may be an even greater problem since the behaviour of other children is likely to be more unpredictable and, therefore, frightening. It is a mistake to expect children with autism to join in with others in free or 'play' times. They will not understand the rules of these unstructured social situations and so the task of 'joining in' becomes even more difficult. It is easier to get social contact with peers if they are engaged in a structured activity together. The best strategy is to give the child with autism pre-training in the task or activity so what they learn from the group is how to do the task with others, while the others are learning to do the task itself.

Negativism

If tasks are within a child's level of competence then less non-cooperative behaviours are observed. We also need to ensure that the child has understood the request or command, before we assume the child is being negative or non-compliant.

Nevertheless, one of the central features of autism is that the individual resists changes in routine and engages in repetitive stereotyped behaviours. The appearance of negativism, therefore, usually emerges when any new behaviour is introduced, although it is not always a form of resistance to the new; it may be a protest at the old and boring. Another feature of autism seems to be a reluctance to repeat things on demand and so a failure to respond to a problem that has been successfully tackled in the past may just be a failure of motivation. There may rarely be genuine cases of negativism but such cases may arise and be maintained by the-interesting effects they produce in the teacher!

The teaching remedy for all these cases will depend on the initial detective work in isolating the 'cause' of the negativism. In most cases the actual remedy is obvious once this has been done. In general, children with autism usually respond best to positive situations where the teacher assumes compliance and the task is structured in such a way that the child understands what to do, where, when, how, and when to finish. We also need to think of the future and how to foster independence and self-assertiveness. To that end we should not make all situations ones where the child has to comply with the wishes or orders of others; we should allow opportunity for choice and for learning to direct the behaviour of others.

We also need to monitor our instructions to the child to make sure they have been understood and remembered. Written or pictorial instructions are usually better than spoken words, but, if we use the latter we must be careful to use short sentences with sufficient pauses in between. Even where individual words and phrases are understood, too long or fast a delivery may be beyond the child's capacity to process and so may be experienced as incomprehensible and increasingly loud. This may be frightening or disturbing or even painful and so will make the child more withdrawn and less likely to join in and cooperate.

Peer relationships

Few people with autism make personal friendships of any depth. Lack of empathy also often results in increasing isolation as they get older. This may seem sad to us, but many people with autism are happy to be on their own. What teachers need to do is to ensure that the child acquires the skills and understanding to make and keep friends so that, if they then choose to be on their own, that is a real choice and not the result of fear or lack of ability.

There needs to be a two-pronged attack on this. One goal for teaching should be the building of friendships and the skills that enable a child to enter a group, maintain the group topic, share information with a group and recognize and talk about things that interest others as well as oneself. For the non-speaking child, this transfers into learning to act with others and to join in with others in co-operative play activities that involve the same kinds of skills.

The other prong to the teaching attack, however, needs to recognize that these skills are not going to be easy for the child to acquire and many may never be achieved at a functional level. Thus, it is necessary to ensure that academic skills are not held back by insistence on learning in collaborative groups and if is necessary to try to teach those aspects of development that would normally be 'picked up' in the course of friendship groups. This will include teaching the adolescent or young adult which rules are important to adhere to at all times and which can sometimes be bent or broken according to circumstances. This is very difficult to achieve but it is important that they learn, for example, that it may be necessary not to fell an adult about a misdemeanour of a friend, as long as there are no serious consequences for the individual him/herself.

When it comes to helping individuals with autism to mix and play with others, if not to truly form friendships, there have been some successes. There are good examples of 'reverse integration' where mainstream children come into the 'autistic' setting to play or work with those with autism, rather than expecting the children with autism to adjust to new settings as well as new people and expectations. Some schools have developed programmes that encourage reliance on peers rather than adults and teaches the outward signs of friendship behaviour at least. It may seem a sham to teach the outward show of friendship without the emotional attachment that usually underpins it, but to have even a superficial friend may serve a valuable function and be a gateway both to a wider social life and to further social understanding.

Teacher/pupil relationship

The process of education is based on the notion that the teacher is a facilitator and mediator of the learning experience. Clearly, if the pupil is disturbed or confused by this social interaction, then this will have tremendous implications for teaching. Good teachers are used to developing a relationship with children as a first step in teaching them and using that relationship to stimulate and motivate the children to further academic learning. Yet in autism that relationship cannot be built in isolation, just through contact, and so teaching and learning cannot depend on its existence. In fact, it may be the case that it is by working regularly with the child on some academic task that the teacher has the best chance of developing that relationship. In other words, the normal teaching sequence may be reversed.

After a while, however, most children with autism will develop relationships with those who make themselves predictable and will learn best from such familiar people. Sometimes they become over dependent on teacher affirmation and approval, however. They may depend on the teacher for confirmation that their responses are appropriate, and to initiate the next stage in any problem-solving process. This sometimes reaches the point where they will not take any action, physical or intellectual, without prior approval. They seem to have no reference point in terms of their own experience, and therefore come to rely on someone else's ability in organizing thoughts and subsequent actions.

There have been special curricular approaches that do not rely on this pupil teacher relationship, either because the teacher does not act in a social way with the child or is not part of the teaching situation. This may be a necessary step in some instances to avoid holding back academic progress, but there should also be a parallel programme of teaching the child how to learn in social contexts. It may be, however, that the teaching situation needs to adjust as much as the child and that some teaching approaches are more facilitory that others. Approaches that rely exclusively on behavioural techniques, for example, may foster this excessive dependency.

ENABLING COMMUNICATION SKILLS OF CHILDREN WITH AUTISM

There are considerable variations in language ability within the autistic population, with some remaining without language throughout life, while others appear to have very good structural language skills, speaking in full sentences, reading and writing well. Yet, regardless of the level of language ability, all children with autism will suffer from a communication disorder.

Language and communication are normally so totally bound together in development that it is hard to envisage the situation in autism, where they take different developmental paths. Whereas communication is the normal precursor to language development, in autism language may develop without the child having any idea of how to use it for communication or any understanding of how speakers can use it pragmatically to create a variety of meanings beyond the literal meaning of the words and sentences. Most children will pay more attention to what they think the speaker intends than to the literal meaning of the language used; children with autism are blind to that intention and focus on the literal meaning regardless of how absurd or unlikely that may appear to be to the onlooker.

Nor is it just the communicative uses and understanding of language that are affected; there are difficulties with all aspects of communication. They are able to hear intonation patterns in speech, for example, but they cannot attach pragmatic meaning to them and so they just become 'noise' that distracts from and interferes with the meaning of what is said, rather than adding to it. They have similar difficulty in using intonation patterns appropriately in their own speech, which then sounds either very monotonous or robot like or has widely variable intonation patterns.

Similar difficulties are experienced in interpreting facial expressions, signs and gestures, body postures and even the regulation of personal space. Pointing in particular, whether through the index finger or through head or eye pointing, is affected. A failure to engage in spontaneous indicative pointing is now considered one of the key indices of possible autism when the child is eighteen months old.

Language Difficulties

Structural aspects of language may only be a problem where there are additional learning or language difficulties. A significant number of individuals with autism remain mute and will need to be taught a means for communication. However, they will have difficulty in learning all language forms without an understanding of communication to support them, so that sign language may be almost as difficult as speech. For most children with autism using pictures or written cards to communicate will be the most helpful strategy. Even children with severe learning difficulties may be able to learn to read in a functional way and this may help them learn to speak as well as being a useful alternative way of communicating for those who remain mute. However good a child's language skills, autism always means there are at least some communication difficulties and such children may still have problems understanding language when it is too complex, when it is too fast or when there is too much else to take in at the same time. For a few children with autistic spectrum disorders, there may also be associated specific language problems such as dyslexia and this will obviously make it difficult in those cases to use reading and writing as an alternative to speech.

Literal language understanding and use

Because of the failure to understand about communication, language tends to be used for a very narrow range of purposes, mainly to make requests and to talk obsessively about some aspect of especial interest. It is often non-productive in the sense that it does not build on what others have said nor does it relate to the context, but tends to reproduce familiar learned patterns of speech. The individual with autism will try to understand what the words mean rather than what the speaker means, she/he will interpret idioms or sarcasm literally and so may miss the point or even become distressed.

Teachers will need to address these problems by direct teaching of conversational skills such as turn taking, active listening, topic introduction, maintenance and change and attempting to make pragmatic knowledge explicit. Turn taking can start with very simple turn-taking games with objects and then, in the pre-verbal child, with games built around mutual imitation. This may start with the adult imitating the noises made by the child and, once the child has noticed this and is pausing to allow the adult turn, gradually changing the sounds made, to encourage the child to pay attention to adult sounds and imitate them.

A more able child with good spoken language will need to learn to turn take and to listen and take account of the turns of others in the context of groups. Passing round an object that signifies that the person holding the conch has the speaker's turn can help regulate turn-taking in a group, although older children will need 'additional practice in recognizing the more natural ways that turn taking is regulated in groups if they are to generalize these skills.

Getting the children to listen to what others say and take account of it in their own speech is more difficult. There are some games which can help with this process. The 'shopping' game has each child saying "I went to the shop and in my basket I put some...'. The first child completes this phrase with his or her own choice ("biscuits' for example) but the next child must now complete the phrase by repeating what the first child said ('biscuits' in this case) and then adding his or her own choice. This goes on round the group with each child having to listen to what has gone before and take account of it in their own answer. Of course, group numbers will need to be small if the task is to be manageable and the game may have to be introduced by having picture cards to register what each child has said and to reduce the demands on memory.

Reading and writing

Some individuals with autism will exhibit what is known as 'hyperlexia' where they are able to read mechanically beyond their level of understanding. The individual with autism may find it easier to learn to read than to listen to stories or to tell them from picture books, so the normal stages in progression may not apply. However, those with associated dyslexia will need special techniques for learning to read.

For most children with autism, teachers will need to check for understanding of read texts and to look for opportunities to demonstrate the purpose of reading.

This is most easily accomplished if the individual is encouraged to read factual texts rather than fantasy stories. Giving children written instructions to complete familiar tasks has the dual function of helping them gain independence in completing the task and helping them learn to read.

The problems of teaching those with additional dyslexia are more complex. Using multi-sensory approaches to teach reading may help as will the use of computer assisted learning. Like many dyslexic children, children with autism may find it easier to remember movement patterns than auditory patterns or, in some cases, visual patterns. It is a good idea, then, to try to teach them proper keyboard skills from the start, rather than typing with one or two fingers as most children (and adults!) will do. This will enable them to learn to spell by repeating the movement pattern with their fingers.

Educational uses of language

There may be failure to appreciate communicative intent so that 'common sense' is never applied to work out what is really meant. This difficulty is not easy to understand and the child's misinterpretation is often attributed to obstinacy or willfulness or a lack of motivation. For much the same reason it may be difficult for the child with autism to understand instructions, especially if these are expressed in indirect 'polite' forms.

Many questions asked in teaching contexts are not 'genuine' in the sense that they seek information that the questioner has not got; rather, they are asked to test the individuals' understanding, to encourage greater individual participation, or to issue instructions. Individuals with autism may mistake these educational uses for the proper use of questions and use it as a model for their own repetitive questioning.

Teachers will need to approach this range of difficulties in two ways. One aspect involves a conscious monitoring of the language they use in instruction to make sure its meaning is clear and does not require an appreciation of what people intend rather than what they say. Teachers will need to restrict their use of sarcasm or irony or even metaphor, although it will seldom be possible to eliminate these forms entirely, especially in mixed settings. Even if it were possible, it would leave the person with autism vulnerable to other people using such forms so teachers must also try to teach understanding at the same time as they restrict their use. In work on metaphors, for example, teachers can start with more transparent forms such the use of 'sunny' to mean happy. Pictures of the sun can be drawn with a happy face and the teacher can explain that we often feel happy when the sun is shining so sometimes we just say 'sunny' when we mean someone is a generally happy person.

Where the metaphor is more obscure it is often best not to try to make sense of it in this way for the person with autism but simply to teach them the metaphorical meaning directly, somewhat as if it were a foreign language. In the same way we can get children to tolerate synonyms. Thus we would tell them directly that their outer garment may be called a 'coat' or a 'jacket' or an 'anorak' and that all these words may refer to the same object. Or we would tell a girl with autism that someone might call them an 'angel' or a 'girl' or 'you' or 'Amy' or 'Amy Smith' and that these would all mean her. But some of these words could be used to refer to other people and some would be more specific to her. Also some would depend on circumstances and contexts so that 'you' would only be used when someone was talking directly to you and 'angel' when someone thought you were being very good. Of course, just telling the child about all these meanings would not help them very much; the teacher will need to show them how they are used in everyday contexts and to draw their attention to ways in which they can use such terms themselves to refer to others.

Facilitated Communication

This is a technique involving a particular form of prompting a child to point to letters or words either on a communication board or with a special computer. The approach is based on the assumption that autism is really a motor disorder and that the person with autism knows what he or she wants to say but cannot execute the motor movements to speak or to type or point independently. A facilitator helps the child to do this by assisting the withdrawal of the pointing finger after it has made a point and re-positioning it for the next point. In this way, many remarkable texts have been 'written' by mute children with autism.

Although there is still a degree of controversy surrounding this approach, it has generated considerable research. There is some concern that facilitators unconsciously prompt the messages being written, but individuals report positive results. Useful side effects from the use of FC in autism include confirming that many children with autism, even with severe learning difficulties, can be taught to read and type, thereby communicating, and reminding staff that many children with autism have additional motor problems and often need help in planning and executing movements. In addition, it provides a context in which staff and/or parents can sit with their child and enjoy a teaching task together. These aspects are positive but those applying the technique should be aware of the danger that unintentional guidance may produce misleading results.

Fostering communication

Where there is little or no understanding of communication, it is not sufficient to teach language skills (whether these are a spoken language, a written language or a system of signs, symbols, pictures or objects). This will just give children the means with which to communicate but, in the case of autism, it will not ensure that they are able to do so. There are at least three essential components to the ability to communicate:

- something to communicate with (a language or a communication system)
- something to communicate about (involving an awareness of one's own needs, desires and intentions and a shared understanding of the world with others)
- something to communicate for (an environment that is responsive to expressed communication and where there is some manageable pressure to communicate)

In autism, there will be an additional need: that of teaching the child what communication is. This means in practical terms that we have to teach children with autism to use whatever means they have to communicate and we have to address all the forms of communication, including the earliest ones of facial expression and gesture. We also need to consider how we can encourage an understanding of communication that will lead to more spontaneous use of whatever language the child has.

Understanding communicative gestures

Parents and teachers need to achieve the discipline of giving explicit instructions of what the child is actually to do, instead of relying on implicit understanding of communication. They will not only need to be told where to look to achieve joint attention but also that holding items up is a signal to direct attention to that object, as is pointing. Direct teaching of the meaning of certain gestures may also be helpful, especially to the more verbally able child.

One of the main difficulties facing teachers of children with autism is knowing how to start teaching them about communication. Because it is normally an intuitive process learnt in the early years of life, it is hard to know how it can be broken down into teachable 'steps'. Below are some suggestions.

Starting the communicative process, by imputing meaning to the child's non-communicative expressions, is the basis of normal language and communication development. Thus the young girl with autism may not have meant to tell anyone that she was hungry when she started to cry and hit herself each morning, but, if the teachers have worked out that that is probably what is wrong, they can treat her behaviour as if that were what it meant.

Each time she starts to cry they can say "Oh! You must be hungry!" and then offer food. After a while, the timing of this can be so the girl only just starts to cry before her need is met. Then she can be prompted to communicate that need in a different way (giving a card to the teacher with a picture of food on it, for example, or giving an 'object of reference' such as a spoon or plate). The success of this programme relies on the teachers working out accurately what it is that the child would want to be communicating in that situation at that time if she knew how.

Imitation of the child's spontaneous actions can also be another strategy for getting the child starting to communicate. It is effective in getting individuals with autism to pay attention to others and learning that they can modify their behaviour. The teacher or parent starts playing a game whereby they copy the child's noises or actions, timing the imitations and the pauses so that the child begins to notice and turn-taking is established. Some children with autism may resist this intrusion into their 'private' actions at first but in time most accept it and begin to like the fact that they have a way of controlling what the adult does. Once this is well established, the adult can begin to change the action or noise a little to see if the child can be persuaded to imitate that, and so begin to acquire the very useful skill of imitation.

For more able pupils who may have some degree of language skills but are still very communicatively impaired, we should look for any communicative intent that might be there or might sensibly be imputed. Where the child is apparently lacking in all attempts at communication, the easiest communicative function to start with is that of request, for this can most readily be demonstrated and it is the first communicative function to develop in autism. But even here teachers and parents must beware of just teaching a 'ritual' that must be gone through first, or just polite conformity.

The individual may be at the stage where outbursts are a simple reaction to need, without communicative intent at all. However, the teacher can use such outbursts to impute the communicative intent of a request and teach the individual to grab; if the individual already tries to grab then the communication training starts there. Teaching the individual to stop and look at the teacher, by interrupting the 'grab' sharply with a restraining hand can be built on until the individual is coming to give that checking look spontaneously as she/he reaches for the item. This can be extended to a variety of contexts and, once it is secure, the grabbing hand can be gradually shaped into a point until the individual has the communicative act of pointing and looking. Teaching pointing, without these preliminaries to teach the meaning, will only lead to meaningless pointing, even when there is no-one in the room to see the point.

Communication Problems in Autism

Conversational skills

Conversation requires spontaneity not only in the production of utterances but in keeping track of the discourse to monitor its progress and actively listen to the contributions of others in order to match one's own utterance in terms of topic relevance, style and timing. This is a complex array of skills which is difficult for children with autism, even when their language skills are apparently good.

Some of the outward forms of conversational behaviour can be taught. Children can be taught to take turns, the rules for entering conversations, ways of changing topic politely and even ways of closing conversations, although that is more difficult. It may even be possible to get children with autism to pay attention to what others are saying but it is far more difficult to teach appropriate timing for these behaviours or the very subtle responsiveness to different circumstances which is the hallmark of fluent behaviour. One way of tackling the problem is to teach sufficient skills to enable the person to begin to participate in conversations with others. It is only through active participation that these more subtle behaviours will ever be acquired.

Understanding and telling stories

This is not just a difficulty in understanding imaginary characters and events, but includes difficulties in remembering the gist of what they hear and telling people about personal events in a meaningful way.

Fictional stories that are read are difficult because it is even harder to understand why people do things if you cannot see the very cues that you have been learning painfully are associated with certain feelings.

Yet some children with autism can become very obsessional about particular stories, especially cartoons, or videos and demand to have the same ones told over and over again. It is not clear what the fascination of these particular ones are but it may be that the characters are simplified humans who do predictable things and have definite characters so that they are less confusing than stories that relate to real people or which are ambiguous about people's motives and beliefs. A more mundane difficulty with story time in school is that it may involve sitting and listening to verbal information at a speed and of a length that the child with autism cannot follow. Nor is the child very clear about what is meant by 'listening' and they will see it as the same as 'hearing', rather than realizing that it involves an active process of trying to make sense of what is heard. Where there are additional problems of hyperactivity, as there often are, it is of little use to exhort the child to 'sit still and listen'; they may need something to do or at least fiddle with, if they are to be able to listen.

Helping children understand that listening is an active process and helping them tolerate sitting to listen to a story can start with being given toy characters or puppets and being taught to act out the main themes of the story being told. For children with written language skills, the structure of a story can be made more explicit by being taught to pick out all the words that refer to the main character (e.g. Rohit, he, his, him) and underline or highlight them in a certain colour. Then other characters can be highlighted using their own colour. Yet another separate colour can be used to highlight the actions of the main character and so on.

Helping children with autism talk about what has happened to them and what they have been doing needs to be tackled in a slightly different way. We can borrow from the techniques of normal child rearing and mimic (and emphasize and adapt) the way in which parents normally help their children learn to talk about themselves through a process of first going over events in a structured way and then prompting them to talk about it in a structured way to others. The structure used consists of questions that help the child see that one needs to talk about a character (who?), an event (what?), a time (when?), a consequence (what then?) and an emotional/experiential reaction (how?). The child is helped to build up this topic-comment structure of a narrative through a careful scaffolding of this kind. For children with autism the scaffolding may need to be more emphatic.

ENCOURAGING FLEXIBILITY IN THINKING AND BEHAVIOUR

Children with autism are often characterized as having behaviour that is 'ritualistic'. They often develop routines on which they then come to rely, so that disturbances in those routines may lead to stress and even challenging behaviour. Another very noticeable feature of rigidity is that children with autism often seem unable to transfer what they have learnt in one situation to another and much of their learning is habitual; they rely on the same cues being present in order to remember and 'trigger' the response.

It is important here to make the distinction between those with different levels of intelligence, and in particular, to the difference that possession of good language skills can make. The rigidity of thought and behaviour is still apparent in high functioning children with autism, although it will manifest itself in more complex ways than in the pupil with autism and additional learning difficulties. Obsessional interests are more a feature of the high functioning group than simple repetitive actions or stereotypes although these too may appear at times of stress. The more profound the additional learning difficulties, the more likely are stereotyped and self-stimulatory activities and this is even more so when there are additional sensory disabilities. Teachers, then, need to adjust their own behaviours so as to make themselves more predictable, to reduce stress and enable a relationship to be established, but they also need to look for ways of helping the children make predictions and learn in less structured situations.

Learning and Behaviour

Children with autism can be taught procedural habits or automatic skills through behavioural methods of training, but real education involves deep learning in which the individual's cognitive structures are altered, and this is the only way in which truly independent learning can be achieved. For children with autism who do not have language, and/or who have additional severe learning difficulties, such independent learning may be difficult to achieve, but this should be an aim, albeit a long-term one.

Children with autism have difficulties in reading the intentions of others but they also have difficulty in developing intentions of their own. It is as hard for them to project themselves forward to make their behaviour goal-directed as it is for them to remember personal events. It is noticeable that it is only when their own obsessional interest is involved that this can serve to make their behaviour focused towards achieving certain ends; it is cognitively difficult for them to direct their behaviour towards some 'other-defined' goal.

Non-autistic children learn what it is to have intentions through early interactions in which they notice and respond to the effects they have on others and direct their behaviour towards producing those effects and collaborating in joint intentions. From those joint intentions comes not only awareness of how to direct one's own behaviour towards ends, but also that this is a feature of the behaviour of others also.

So, children with autism will tend to learn in a habitual kind of way without any real awareness of, or ability to monitor, that learning. This means they become dependent on others to cue or prompt them and the behaviour pattern is disrupted if any part of it is changed or interrupted. This explains why more able youngsters with autism who are interrupted in a long monologue about an obsessional interest or in the process of a routine, will have to start again from the beginning, rather than being able to take it up again from the interrupted point. It also explains why less able children with autism will have no idea how to clean their teeth in their grandmother's house, for example, if they have only been taught to do so in their own home. The performance of the skill is dependent on the right cues to trigger it, and, once triggered, it has to run its course.

Intuitive *Versus* Learned Behaviours

As with so much in autism, however, it is not so much that the child with autism cannot do things as that play and interests do not develop spontaneously and, if they are directly 'taught', they tend to remain limited to the kinds of play and interests that have been demonstrated. Again, the more able child may display imagination, but it is likely to be of a limited kind, and there may be difficulty then in distinguishing imagination from reality. With some individuals it is as if there is no basis for distinguishing mental images from images produced directly from the environment.

Cognitive Difficulties in Autism

Perception

There are many reports of inconsistency or fluctuating perception in autism and many high functioning individuals writing personal accounts of autism attribute their difficulties to a mixture of perceptual or sensory integration difficulties. It may be difficult to distinguish cause and effect in thinking of the nature of these difficulties. Is it a problem in processing rapid information that leads to difficulties in interpreting social meaning, or difficulties in 'tuning in' emotionally to others that leads to social isolation and consequently to a failure to categorize and understand the world?

At a practical level, understanding that a child may be over or undersensitive to particular forms of stimulation can be helpful in explaining extreme reactions or indeed lack of reaction. It also helps the member of staff to realize that perceptions may vary from one extreme to the other even within the course of a day, although it may then be more difficult to find a solution. It is also important for teachers to be aware that integration of stimuli may not only be difficult of itself but may require extra time.

If children with autism are oversensitive to general stimulation, then a low intrusion approach to their learning environment and teaching approach will be of benefit. Bright lights may need to be reduced, noises deadened with soft flooring, visual displays all but removed and the teacher will need to speak minimally in a low or even whispered voice. Such an extreme environment will not be necessary for all children with autism and even those who start in such a way may be gradually reintroduced to a more natural environment through a process of desensitization. Reducing stimulation can have a dramatic effect in reducing the child's stress and making him or her more receptive to learning.

However, if the problem is one of variable sensitivity rather than just over-sensitivity, it is difficult to deal with imply in this way. Carers or teachers would need to give some proximal control device to the individual such as ear plugs (or a 'Walkman' radio) or coloured lenses so that the child can use them as and when needed. Just having control can do a lot to reduce the fear and anxiety provoked by over stimulation and consequently can have a marked effect on behaviour. Sensory integration may be tackled through sensory integration programmes and allowing the child to use proximal senses such as touch for exploration of objects. This can apply even to the most able whose verbal and academic skills may mask this underlying confusion in interpreting the world. There is also the need to give the child time to process his or her environment and teaching styles and curriculum delivery must allow for this.

Attention

When teachers describe a child with autism as having a 'short attention span' they usually mean that the child will fail to concentrate on the tasks the teacher has set. In some cases this may be a problem of motivation where the child does not understand the purpose of the task nor see the need to 'please the teacher'. However, attentional problems in autism are not all due to this kind of motivational problem and there may be genuine difficulties in sustaining attention, especially when the child is young. It is also clear that children with autism have problems in switching attention and may take a long time to do so; the danger is that the teacher will not wait long enough for a response and may rephrase the instruction, giving another processing task on top of the first.

There are many reports in the literature of people with autism attending to detail but not being able to see the whole. This is undeniably true in some instances but it appears to relate to what is seen as meaningful rather than an invariable feature of cognitive style. It was also thought that individuals with autism were unable to attend to more than one stimulus at a time, but this is probably a developmental delay rather than a deficit. Many individuals with autism will be unable to attend to two sources of information at the same time which means that instructions or commands only serve to enhance (rather than direct) the actions the individual is already performing; unless this is understood, the individual may be seen as 'disobedient' rather than having a problem with processing.

The most well-documented attentional problem in autism, however, is that relating to 'joint attention' which is at the heart of the interpersonal difficulties. It is not that children with autism are unable to follow where someone is looking if they are instructed to do so, but rather that they do not do so spontaneously and so they miss out on all the shared referencing that is the foundation for social, cognitive and cultural development. It may also be that this failure to attend to social and cultural meanings leads to greater attention being devoted to proximal senses than is normally the case, so that responses to others may be very dependent on how others smell, feel or taste more than how they look or what they say.

One lesson for teachers is to ensure that the intended focus of attention must be made meaningful to the individual with autism. This can be done by drawing attention to the child's natural activity, rather than always expecting the child to pay attention to the topic the teacher has chosen. Sharing activities, whether this is working together at a computer or playing an imitation game involving one of the child's stereotypic actions, may also be effective. When it is important to gain the child's attention, staff will need to make sure the child is not doing anything else and to give sufficient time for the child to switch attention. Joint attention cannot be assumed and so instructions to "Look at what I am holding/ pointing to/ looking at' will need to be given explicitly.

A failure to appreciate social and emotional meaning may also help explain the difficulty in focusing attention on some aspects of the stimulation being received while ignoring others. This means the child may not be able to attend selectively to the teacher talking when there is other competing noise or may not be able to sit still if the feel of the clothes on the skin or the chair on the bottom makes it hard for them to think of anything else. In the visual domain also, it means that the child may need a relatively display-free area in which to work, at least for new or concentrated learning. It also means that 'talking a child through a task', as is common practice in schools, may make it more difficult for the individual with autism to concentrate on that task. Teachers may need to look for ways of structuring the task so that the child knows what to do, when and how without the need for additional instruction. Good practice will draw the child's attention to the way in which things are related in a very deliberate way and try to help the child see the patterns.

Memory

There are often very good rote memories and amazing recall of detail alongside an inability to give the gist of a story or event and an apparent failure to remember what happened to themselves even a short while before. Memories need to be cued or prompted in some way and there appears to be no way in which individuals with autism can search and produce memories spontaneously.

Thus, it is not that they have completely 'forgotten', or that they are deliberately not co-operating; they just do not find it easy to retrieve memories, especially related to general prompts concerning what they have done in the past.

Children with autism may be able to recall facts about themselves, and episodes that do not include a personal element. They may also be able to recall particular episodes when they are cued by particular words or phrases or by being in exactly the same situation again. In fact, such memories may not be under conscious control and may be triggered by the environment at inopportune moments leading to inappropriate behaviour and delayed echolalia. Children with autism may also have little difficulty in remembering particular aspects of 'general knowledge', especially related to their own particular interests.

They are also likely to have good procedural knowledge for skills, such as bicycle riding or playing a musical instrument. But at the same 56 time as all of this they may be unable to remember themselves performing actions, participating in events or possessing knowledge and strategies. This means that they are dependent on others providing them with the right cues to get them started and any disruption of a learned way of tackling a task will mean the child is completely at a loss as to how to proceed.

Awareness of these difficulties will help the teacher draw the individual's attention to relevant features at the time of learning which can serve as cues at the time of recall. They will also need to be taught how to use semantic strategies to memorize rather than relying on remembering 'snatches' of events. For example, music is often important to children with autism so a musical phrase can be used to describe an event at the time so that the rhythm mirrors the actions and the key words to remember are emphasized in the musical stress. Then, when asked to recall later what he had made in cookery, the music can be played or hummed as a trigger for him to sing the song and so recall the event.

A child with more language skills might be taught to use the scaffolding questions. Instead of waiting for the teacher to prompt with "who?, what? when? how?" questions, the child can be taught to use them him or herself to cue the structure of the event and aid memory. In trying to get a child to tell about a past event shared with others, it may also be helpful to ask the child what others did or what happened to others, as this seems to be easier for them to recall, from the 'outside' as it were, rather than trying to retrieve personal memories.

Teachers also need to use the natural environmental cues to aid memory. After a task has been completed, for example, the child has painted a picture, the child should be asked to recall the event while there are still clues to trigger the memory. In that case the clues might come from paint on the child's hands, from the apron used, and so on. This initial discussion before the child has cleared up can be reinforced later after clearing up so that the child's memories begin to be triggered by internal cues, but this needs to be managed slowly. At first, the teacher may still need to jog the memory by reintroducing the painting apron, for example, even though the child is no longer wearing it.

Problem-solving

In common with many others with learning difficulties and especially those with poor language skills, children with autism display poor metacognitive skills. These difficulties mean that children with autism often learn in a rote way, adhere to learned responses in certain situations and are at a loss if the response does not work. They find it very difficult to inhibit their actions and will persist with habitual responses even when these are known to be wrong or when they are punished. They cannot model their own intentions, which leads to apparent motivational problems and they rely on others or the situation to cue their actions. It also means they will have difficulty making choices or even understanding what a choice is and an inability to benefit from "incidental learning' where particular responses have not been trained.

If it is important that the child achieves a certain skill or performs a certain activity then it is important to structure them in such a way that the problem-solving element is reduced to a minimum. A goal of long-term independence, however, requires consistent attempts to teach the child to become aware of the process of learning and the stages of problem-solving.

Choice should be introduced into as many situations as possible in ways that are meaningful to the child and which offer structured alternatives to begin with. Thus, a child may be taught to use pictures to indicate a choice so that the choosing situation can be one of selecting from an array of pictures, rather than being confronted with real items. The advantage of this is that, in the real situation, the child may only notice the item wanted and may point to that without being aware of the alternatives, and so is not really aware of making a choice at all. It may also be difficult for children to inhibit their responses to items and so using a distal stimulus may help them make a real choice.

All teaching should involve a period of planning where the child is taught to intend by selecting what is needed for the task and having a clear idea of the goal to be aimed at. At one level, the child with severe learning difficulties and no speech, who is asked to lay the table, will need a photograph of how the table will look when finished. This will not only make the goal clear and specific, and help keep the child on task, but it can be used at the planning stage to help the child plan the task by first counting and assembling all the items needed (e.g. six forks, six mats, six glasses, etc.) before arranging them.

Concept acquisition

Children with autism do not seem able to see the meaningful patterns in the world around them and have difficulty analysing stimulation and abstracting the features that lead to concepts being formed. More able individuals will talk about their problems in thinking in conceptual terms. Sometimes this is described in the literature as a difficulty with abstract concepts but, if we listen to what people with autism tell us, we find that they are having just as much difficulty in thinking about a 'chair', or a 'cat' as they have thinking about 'old' or even 'peace' or 'justice'.

They have to think in terms of particular experiences, thinking about a particular chair or cat, an old man, a peaceful scene, a judge in a wig and gown. Of course the effect will be more noticeable when it comes to abstract concepts since a judge in a wig and gown is more misleading about the concept of justice than a particular chair is about the concept of a chair. Yet all these rigid concepts will inhibit thinking and will be harder to elaborate and link together than would be more flexible concepts.

Although we do not normally acquire concepts by a logical analysis of their features this may be one step forward in helping some more able children with autism extend their concepts. For less able children, however, and for all children with autism in the early years, we need to adopt a particular teaching approach. The child is not taught about a particular object or procedure, and then has to 'unlearn' its particularity while learning a more general concept, e.g, learn that a particular cup is 'a cup' and then learn that there are, in fact, lots of kinds of cup. Instead, the broader concept would be introduced from the beginning, teaching the child to pay attention to 'meaning' from the start, e.g. the child would learn that various shapes and sizes of cup can be used for drinking from, and only then, that they are all called 'cup'.

Generalization

There is a well-established difficulty in transferring knowledge and skills to new situations. Those with spoken language will find it easier to learn a generalized 'idea' of the task which can help that transfer; others may have to have more specific cues. Whether this 'bridge' from one task to another is through a language or a symbol system, it cannot be assumed that it will occur naturally, even in the most able.

Important life skills are often taught in a functional context to bypass this problem of generalization. Tackling it may be at different levels. Behavioural strategies do not attack the underlying problems but can be used to encourage transfer, with the child being taught to generalize in a structured way:

- the task is taught with the criterion for success being accuracy.
- there is a period of 'overlearning' where the child learns to do the same task in the same situation with the same materials but with the criteria of success being speed and fluency, while retaining accuracy
- variation is gradually introduced along a range of dimensions (one at a time): different materials, different settings, different times, with different teachers, with different peers, and so on, while retaining the previous criteria of success.

More fundamental gain in this area, however, can only really occur if children are taught to become aware of their own learning strategies, i.e. through self-reflection. With spoken language children can be taught specifically to label what they are doing, both in terms of the overall 'idea' and the steps in the process. They can also be taught to 'rehearse' some of the other contexts in which the task can be generalized.

This is more difficult without language but children can have their photographs taken at every stage in the task and these can be used both to structure the performance of the task, but also to aid memory of it and transfer it to other situations.

Drawings may help, where a camera is not available, but there may need to be training to help the child make the connection between the task or the step in the task and the picture.

Learning about Thinking

A difficulty with mental states and being aware of one's own thinking does not just mean a difficulty in understanding people but also problems in understanding thinking at all. Thus, children with autism are often unaware that tasks require an 'attitudinal stance' in that they have to make an effort to learn or remember.

Retaining a mental image

Teachers need to be aware of the difficulty experienced even by the most able in holding onto a mental image while faced with competing stimuli. This means that even a simple task such as copying a sequence of coloured pegs will often be attempted by the child picking up a handful of pegs and putting them in on an ad hoc matching basis. This may be interpreted as a difficulty in maintaining left to right sequencing, but is more likely to be because the task requires the child to hold the concept of the particular colour next in sequence while searching through a box of pegs with distracters of many different colours.The teacher may need to give the child some more concrete way of retaining the mental image, appropriate to the child's ability. In the peg sequencing task above, for example, this might be simply to repeat the name of the colour being sought during the searching, or to write it down or to have a symbol card to refer to when searching the box. The number of distracters in the box can also be manipulated so that, to begin with, there may be only one and then distracters are added as the child shows understanding of the task.

Integrating thinking

Children with autistic spectrum disorders do not seem to setup models or schema of events they are engaged in or of stories they are told. They do not attend to overall meaning or see the pattern through which things are related. This means that learning becomes fragmented and tied to contexts since the overall meaning is missed and not related to other aspects of the child's knowledge or understanding.

Helping the child understand about thinking can be tackled at one level by teaching the child to follow the main events of a story by acting them out with puppets as the story progresses. This also helps the child tolerate 'story time' since it now has structure and a beginning and an end that can be predicted. A more able child may be taught how events in a narrative relate together by highlighting written texts or giving systematic training in the structure of narratives.

General teaching tasks will need to be analysed to see where children are being asked to reflect on their own mental images, and to see if this is then a barrier to learning. Ways of making the implicit thinking explicit will need to be developed. One attempt at this might be through familiar songs or rhymes in which words are substituted with pauses and the song is rejoined at the correct point, showing that others, like oneself, can be 'thinking' the same things.

Developing creativity

The kind of rigidity of thought that we see in autism seems to run contrary to any notion of creativity. We know that individual children may sometimes produce works that are 'pleasing', but we need to ask if those works are productive or merely reproductive. The distinction that we need to make is whether or not original stimuli have been extended, elaborated or changed by the individual. If they have not, then the work is 'parasitic' in that it derives directly from the original without any intervention at the cognitive level. That is not to decry the achievement inherent in such works or their beauty, but we should not confuse a remarkable ability to recreate what is seen with the creative imagination needed for a more abstract or symbolic form of art.

If we shift the focus beyond 'creative works' to the creative aspects of everyday life, then it seems that children with autism are seldom creative in the sense given above. In every aspect of their lives from their use of language to the way in which they go about activities they will tend to operate within fairly constrained repetitive cycles. If they say or do something that appears to be 'new' or 'inventive' then one needs to check back to sources. Typically, it may be that they are reproducing faithfully chunks of remembered dialogue or actions from a source such as a television programme.

4

EDUCATION OF STUDENTS WITH VISUAL IMPAIRMENTS

Visual impairment refers to a significant loss of vision, even though the person may wear corrective lenses. The nature and degree of visual impairment may vary significantly, so each student may require individual adaptations to instructional practices and materials in order to learn effectively.

CATEGORIES OF VISUAL IMPAIRMENT

Visual impairment includes two main categories: blindness and low vision.

- *Legal Blindness*: Legal blindness ranges from a visual acuity of 20/200 in the better eye after correction, to having no usable vision or a field of vision reduced to an angle of 20 degrees. Visual acuity of 20/200 means that the individual sees at 20 feet what is normally seen at 200 feet. A reduced field of vision means that the individual has tunnel vision with limited peripheral vision.
- *Blindness*: Blindness ranges from being totally without sight to unreliable vision and primary reliance on other senses. A person with blindness

usually uses braille as a reading and writing medium.

- *Low Vision:* Low vision is reduced central acuity of 20/70 or less in the better eye after correction. Most students with visual impairments have low vision. These students should be encouraged to use their residual (remaining) vision, when appropriate, using the necessary optical aids and adaptations. Students who are described as blind may have some usable vision.

Visual impairments are further classified as congenital or adventitious.

- *Congenital* refers to loss of vision present at birth. Some of the more common causes of congenital visual impairment are:
    - prematurity;
    - genetic diseases;
    - prenatal and perinatal infections; and
    - maternal substance abuse.
- *Adventitious* refers to loss of vision acquired after birth as a result of illness or accident.

The age and level of development of the student before the onset of the visual impairment influences the student's ability to acquire skills and concepts. Students with congenital blindness may have difficulty acquiring concepts, while students with adventitious blindness may retain sufficient visual memory to benefit from visual descriptions.

Although two students may be medically assessed as having the same diagnosis and visual acuity, they may each learn and function in different ways. A student's vision may fluctuate or may be temporarily influenced by such factors as:

- the nature of the visual impairment;
- fatigue;
- glare;
- inappropriate lighting;
- medication; and
- general health.

COMMON EYE CONDITIONS

Following are the most common eye conditions teachers may encounter.

Albinism

Albinism is a genetic condition in which there is a lack of normal pigment in the eyes and often in the skin and hair. Students with albinism usually have reduced visual acuity, sensitivity to light and nystagmus.

Amblyopia

Amblyopia is referred to as a lazy eye. There is reduced visual functioning in one eye that causes the student to use only one eye instead of both.

Cataract

A cataract is an opacity or cloudiness of the lens of the eyes, sometimes present at birth. Students with cataracts have reduced visual acuity and hazy vision that makes near and distant visual activities difficult, particularly in bright light. They may have poor colour discrimination.

Cortical Visual Impairment

Cortical visual impairment is caused by damage to the visual cortex in the brain or the nerve pathways. Most students with cortical visual impairment also have other disabilities. The visual response from students with cortical visual impairment is inconsistent. Providing visual stimulation may improve the student's ability to process visual input.

Retinal Detachment

A retinal detachment occurs when parts of the retina pull away from the supporting structure of the eye and atrophy occurs. The retina may be reattached if little time has transpired.

Glaucoma

Glaucoma is a disease in which there is damage to the optic nerve, through increased pressure from the fluid within the eye, resulting in reduced visual acuity and loss of peripheral vision. The fluid pressure is monitored regularly by an ophthalmologist. Students with glaucoma generally have difficulty with mobility and focusing their gaze between near and distant objects.

Hyperopia

Hyperopia (farsightedness) is a condition in which the rays of light entering the eye focus behind the retina instead of on the retina. Students with hyperopia can see more clearly at a distance.

Macular Degeneration

Macular degeneration is an eye disease which results in gradual loss of central vision. Students with macular degeneration have difficulty reading print on the blackboard or page.

Myopia

Myopia (near sightedness) is a condition in which the rays of light entering the eye focus in front of the retina instead of on the retina. Students with myopia can see more clearly up close.

Nystagmus

Nystagmus is involuntary movement of the eyes that can cause fatigue when carrying out visual tasks. Nystagmus is associated with many eye conditions or it may be the only diagnosis identified by an ophthalmologist.

Optic Atrophy

Optic atrophy is the degeneration of the optic nerve fibers so that they are no longer able to transmit accurate visual images from the retina to the brain. An ophthalmologist will sometimes describe a student as having pale or grey optic disks in one or both eyes, which is an indication of optic atrophy. It is important to determine just how well the student can interpret what is seen both up close and at a distance.

Retinitis Pigmentosa

Retinitis pigmentosa is a hereditary condition in which the retinal cells degenerate, particularly the rods which are responsible for peripheral and night vision. This results in a progressive narrowing of the field of vision, night blindness and often extreme sensitivity to light. Students with retinitis pigmentosa have difficulty with mobility, scanning the environment and reading print on the blackboard or page.

Retinopathy of Prematurity

Retinopathy of prematurity is a disease of the retina in which the retinal blood vessels do not develop normally and scar tissue forms. Most students with retinopathy of prematurity benefit from the use of high illumination and magnifying aids.

Strabismus

Strabismus is a muscle imbalance that prevents the eyes from focusing together on a single point to achieve binocular vision. Students with strabismus may have significantly decreased vision in one eye and have difficulty with depth perception.

NEEDS AND EXPECTATIONS OF STUDENTS WITH VISUAL IMPAIRMENTS

It is essential that students with visual impairments:

- Be made welcome and given the opportunity to form social relationships within the school and wider community;
- Be challenged to take risks that enable growth;
- Be made aware of personal strengths, talents, learning styles and interests;
- Have opportunities for experiential and incidental learning;
- Be included in discussions;
- Have opportunities to develop goals, dreams and aspirations;
- Feel safe and comfortable throughout the school;
- Work with individuals who understand the educational implications of vision loss;
- Have appropriate learning resources and technology made available;
- Be provided with appropriate materials and adaptive equipment to maximize learning;
- Be provided with daily opportunities to experience success; develop positive self-esteem;
- Have the same rights and responsibilities as other students;

- Be expected to behave appropriately;
- Communicate effectively;
- Become independent and resourceful;
- Plan early for meaningful careers; and
- Become self-advocates.

EDUCATIONAL IMPLICATION OF VISUAL IMPAIRMENT

Students with visual impairments sometimes have fewer natural learning experiences because they are not able to observe objects and interactions. The areas of learning which are particularly affected are:

- concept development;
- interpersonal communication skills;
- life skills;
- orientation and mobility skills; and
- academic development.

Development of concepts is the basis of all learning. Spatial relationships, time, body awareness and self-awareness are just a few examples of fundamental concepts individuals need to make sense of their world. These concepts may need to be specifically taught to students with visual impairments. Although the main focus will be on academic development, providing a variety of opportunities for personal development can have a profound impact on a student who is visually impaired. Encouraging a positive self-image, appropriate dress, well-developed self-care skills, good interpersonal communication, appropriate behaviours, increased independence and productive community living can all be tremendously beneficial in the healthy growth of students with visual impairments. As with all students, relationships are important for students with visual impairments and the classroom can be a wonderful place for development and maturity to flourish.

The development of a student with a visual impairment is affected by:

- the type and severity of the visual impairment;
- the onset of the visual impairment;
- the nature and degree of intervention;
- the use of residual vision;
- personality;
- the availability of equipment and resources;
- the presence of other disabilities;
- family adjustment and acceptance; and
- cultural attitudes to visual impairment.

ASSESSMENT

The teacher in obtaining a comprehensive overview of student information in the following areas:

- medical;
- functional vision; and
- educational.

This form provides a guided process for reviewing student files and may be used as an information base in the development of the student's programme plan. It may be completed in consultation with an educational consultant for students with visual impairments.

To facilitate the gathering of information, the student, parent and resource personnel may be interviewed by the teacher.

Students with visual impairments should undergo examinations by ophthalmologists and/or optometrists to determine the nature and degree of the visual impairment. An eye report should be requested from the eye specialist and included in the cumulative records. The educational consultant for students with visual impairments will interpret the medical report for school personnel and identify the educational implications.

Functional Vision Assessment

The educational consultant for students with visual impairments develops a profile of the student's visual skills through a functional vision assessment. This profile, which conveys a picture of how the student sees, will assist the support team in developing the student's programme plan and in augmenting teaching strategies.

A variety of assessment techniques and measures are used in the student's learning environment to determine how vision is used and what adaptations may be necessary. They include:

- file review;
- student observation;
- interviews with parent and teachers;
- play-based assessment;
- performance-based assessment;
- assessment portfolios;
- developmental checklists; and
- assessment tools for determining:
- visual acuity, the finest detail the eye can see at near and far distances;
- visual fields, the student's degree of peripheral vision;
- depth perception, the student's degree of binocular vision (which is the ability of both eyes to work together);

- colour vision;
- appropriate reading and writing media (print, braille, audio); and
- appropriate technological aids and devices.

A functional vision checklist should be repeated when the student makes the transition to a different school or classroom setting or on the recommendation of the educational consultant for students with visual impairments. Growth and maturity can affect the student's vision and the underlying visual impairment may change with time.

Support Team

Team building creates enthusiasm, trust and mutual support, which in the long-term, leads to more effective and efficient task accomplishment. Preparation, planning and cooperation build the framework for learning. Establishing good communication with students, parents, community and school personnel will foster the student's social, emotional, communicative and educational development.

There is often a range of support services required for the student with a visual impairment. It is important to have a contact person in the school designated to coordinate the student's programme. The support team may include the:

- student;
- parents;
- classroom teacher(s);
- special education/resource teacher;
- school administrator;
- teacher assistant(s) ;
- educational consultant for students with visual impairment;

- eye specialist;
- orientation and mobility specialist;
- technology specialist;
- school counsellor;
- early interventionist;
- school division coordinator for students with special needs;
- substitute teacher; and
- related service providers.

Responsibilities of Team members

The school administrator assigns a teacher, usually the special education/resource teacher, the primary responsibility for coordinating and developing the student's individualized programme. Staff develop programme plans with the assistance of parents and, where appropriate, students and other professionals. Listed below are some of the responsibilities and ways in which support team members might participate in the development and implementation of a successful programme plan.

Student

Although the nature and degree of involvement will vary depending on the student and his/her age, the student should be involved in his/her programme plan. The student should:

- understand the purpose of the support team and programme plan and how to take part in the process;
- be encouraged to attend programme planning meetings when appropriate;

- be able to identify, label and explain his/her goals;
- understand how objectives are individually tailored, evaluated, reviewed and updated;
- take responsibility for tracking goals, where appropriate; and
- develop self advocacy skills.

Parents

Education is viewed as the shared responsibility of the home and the school. Parents should be included as active members of the support team as early in the process as possible. Educational priorities identified by family members should be a primary consideration. The benefits of involving parents are numerous. Parents

- are able to communicate a picture of the life of the student thus far;
- can provide up-to-date medical information;
- can help achieve continuity of programming over time;
- have important information regarding the likes, dislikes, interests and skills;
- the child demonstrates in the home and community;
- can assist in developing goals and effective strategies; and
- can offer opportunities for practice, reinforcement, generalization and maintenance of skills in the home.

Strategies to support parent involvement

- communicate openly and regularly with parents in language which is free of jargon;
- clarify how parents can participate;

- give parents the opportunity to specify how, and to what degree, they wish to become involved in the child's educational programme;
- if available, provide parents access to parenting programs and support groups; contact parents by telephone as well as through written communication to notify them of support team meetings and invite them to bring a support person if they wish;
- advise parents of the topics which will be discussed at the support team meetings and who will be in attendance;
- send home a rough draft of goals and objectives to enable parents to familiarize themselves prior to the meeting;
- consider giving parents a goal-setting form that may be used to develop the student's programme plan;
- have a school representative greet the parents, guide them to the conference room and make introductions;
- ensure parents are comfortable at the team meeting; and
- clarify, if you suspect that the parent is concerned or confused about any part of the meeting and summarize the action plan.

Classroom Teacher

The classroom teacher is key to planning and implementing an effective educational programme. The classroom teacher:

- shares information collected during the information gathering stage;

- is aware of the parents' or guardians' expectations for their child's programme;
- is aware of the needs of a student with a visual impairment;
- plans and carries out instructional programs;
- modifies instructional methods and materials allowing ample time for preparation of adapted resources;
- develops strategies for assessing and communicating student progress; and
- maintains ongoing communication with the student, parents and other teachers.

Special Education/Resource Teacher

The resource teacher is usually the teacher designated to coordinate the student's programme. In addition the resource teacher:

- provides diagnostic assessment to determine student strengths and areas of need;
- generates ideas and suggestions for programme modification and/or adaptations;
- provides advice about materials and resources;
- plans and carries out instructional programmes;
- develops strategies for assessing and communicating student progress;
- maintains ongoing communication with parents and other teachers; and
- initiates and organizes support team meetings.

School Administrator

The administrator is a member of the support team. He/She ensures that programme plans are prepared, implemented and evaluated. The administrator ensures support personnel, appropriate materials and in-service training are provided as required, given the needs of the student. The administrator is often the person who can ensure that team decisions can be implemented.

The administrator serves an important leadership function as a good role model by:

- accepting the student in the school;
- legitimizing team decisions;
- including the student in school activities;
- welcoming parental involvement; and
- supporting best practices.

The administrator's role also includes that of programme evaluator and supervisor of staff.

School Counsellor

The role of the school counsellor is to provide counselling services to a student who may be experiencing difficulty accepting his/her visual impairment.

Teacher Assistant

The teacher assistant is part of the support team. The primary responsibility of the teacher assistant is to support the classroom teacher, enabling the teacher to provide an educational programme that meets the needs of all the students in the class, including the student with a visual impairment. It is important to define the role of the teacher assistant. The teacher assistant needs to be sensitive to the interactions between the student and peers, facilitating these relationships and the natural support that peers can provide. Supporting the student with a visual impairment who uses braille as a reading mode, involves becoming proficient in the use of braille. Other tasks may include:

- preparing braille, large print, audio or tactile materials;
- facilitating the student's use of optical and technological aids;
- adapting the environment to meet the student's needs;
- acting as a scribe and a braille transcriber;
- assisting in concept development, organizational and social skills;
- working individually with the student to reinforce the specialized skills, such as orientation and mobility and life skills; and
- serving as an intervener between the student and the environment.

CLASSROOM ACCOMMODATION OF STUDENT WITH LOW VISION

Students with low vision exhibit a wide range of visual impairments. Teachers should be aware that no two students with low vision have the same functional vision even if they are diagnosed as having the same eye condition and similar acuity. Vision may fluctuate and be influenced by such factors as fatigue, light glare, lighting conditions and time of day. Therefore, special attention must be given in assessing the needs of the student with low vision. Accommodations can be incorporated into his/her programme plan.

This section of the chapter presents guidelines for students with low vision at preschool, elementary and secondary levels. The levels at which basic skills and accommodations need to be developed are not discrete. The skills developed in the preschool years will flow into the elementary and secondary years. There are also general guidelines for teaching students with low vision that apply to all levels.

Welcoming the Student

- Introduce the student with low vision as you would any other student.
- Encourage the student to answer questions posed by other students about the eye condition.
- Verbalize praise and disapproval or use gestures such as a hand on the shoulder. Students with low vision may miss the message sent with facial expressions and body language.
- Be specific with descriptive language when explaining the location of a person or object.
- Talk directly to the student, using direct eye contact. Encourage the student to look at you when being addressed or when speaking to you.
- Encourage the student to look directly at people when conversing with them.
- Provide the student with the coat hook or locker closest to the door so it is easy to locate.

Safety

Students with visual impairments face an extra challenge when travelling around the school building. Most areas of the school present potential problems. Procedures such as fire drills, changing classes, going to the library and assemblies require that a plan of action be in place. Assess each room that the student will be using for potential hazards. These suggestions will help provide a safe environment.

- Familiarize the student with the school building as soon as possible.

- Limit clutter in the hallways, stairs and classrooms that the student will be using.
- Students with low vision should become familiar with the location of all furniture and fixtures in the room. If furniture must be relocated, be sure to inform the student.
- Highlight the edges of stairs and steps with contrasting coloured tape or paint.
- Train teachers and other students in the sighted guide technique.
- When going on a field trip or travelling in an unfamiliar environment, arrange for a buddy.

Seating

The seating in the classroom will depend on the functional vision of the student.

- Usually a student with a visual impairment will sit in the front of the classroom to be in closer proximity to the teacher and board.
- If the right eye is stronger, being on the left side of the classroom is best and *vice versa*.
- Source of lighting needs to be considered. A student with a visual impairment should not face direct light from windows or lighting.
- If the student uses a reading stand or tilt-topped desk, be sure the desk provides for good posture to decrease fatigue. The student's feet should be flat on the floor and the reading stand tilted so that the student does not have to bend his/her neck uncomfortably.
- For group activities such as story time or videos, the student may require preferential seating.

- A sound field system may be considered for amplification of the teacher's voice and reduction of extraneous noises.

Teaching Tips

- A programme plan is usually developed on an annual basis by the student's support team and is reviewed regularly.
- Plan ahead. If a student with low vision requires enlarged texts, audiocassettes or printed materials, they should be ordered or prepared ahead of time.
- Talk while you teach. The student may miss visual cues and written instructions.
- Teach in close proximity to the student when doing demonstrations or using visual aids.
- Allow the student to go up to the board or move the desk closer in order to view or copy the material.
- Check regularly to ensure that the student is making accurate notes.
- Provide extra time to the student. He/she will take longer to complete most tasks. The quantity of work required may be decreased.
- Consider oral exams or a scribe to write exam answers.
- Use tactile, concrete and real life material as much as possible. This provides opportunities for kinesthetic and tactile learning.
- Sufficient desktop and shelf space is needed to accommodate special materials. The student will need to learn to organize his/her notes, desk, shelves and locker. Colour coding notebooks and files may help.

- Alternate visual tasks with non-visual tasks to avoid eye fatigue.
- The student with low vision requires the same discipline and behaviour expectations as other students.
- Say, "Tell me what you see" rather than "Can you see this?" when checking if a student can see specific visual material.
- Try to relate new learning to the student's experiences and knowledge. This will help to bridge gaps in learning.
- If a large volume of reading is required, consider having a teacher assistant or another student read the material to the student, or obtain it on audio tape.
- Skip the non-essentials. Older students can highlight important information in print material. Point out parts of the text that can be skipped.
- Provide outlines, point form notes, identify key concepts to help avoid fatigue and frustration when studying.
- The student with low vision may need extra explanation of some materials.
- Hand-over-hand techniques work well to demonstrate certain skills.
- Encourage the student to be assertive. He/she needs to learn when and how to request and refuse help and how to make his/her needs known.
- Encourage independent effort and incorporate proactive measure to reduce the likelihood of the student becoming dependent on others.
- The student's ability to participate in certain activities such as physical education, science labs

and visual arts may be affected by his/her functional vision. Modification may be required.

Assignments and Examinations

Assignments and examinations can pose considerable difficulty for the student with low vision. Examination results should reflect the student's knowledge of the subject content. Each student's individual needs require consideration. The student may take more time to complete an assignment or examination than other students. Consider the student's well-being when assigning homework, particularly if it requires extensive reading or writing. A student with low vision is often fatigued by the end of the school day and work quality may be reduced. Some of the following strategies may be used to enhance a work quality.

- Allow additional time for completion of assignments and examinations.
- Allow the student to complete an examination in more than one sitting if necessary.
- Reduce the number of examples required to demonstrate the student's understanding of a concept or mathematics operation.
- Reduce the number of questions to be answered.
- Provide an alternate way of testing the student's knowledge.
- Give the examination orally. Accept a computer print-out or answers recorded on an audiocassette.

SUGGESTIONS FOR TEACHING STUDENTS WITH LOW VISION

Mathematics

- Students with low vision must physically manipulate concrete materials to master the basic concepts of math.

- The basic concepts of addition, subtraction, multiplication and division should be thoroughly understood before being practised on the abacus or talking calculator.
- Practice mental math skills.
- Provide a compartmentalized tray in which to place articles for counting and matching.
- Pictorial directions for young students are helpful.
- Demonstrate measuring instruments individually to students with low vision.
- When doing activities involving measuring, the units used should be sufficiently large so that the student can work without assistance.
- Provide a worksheet instead of having the student copy from the board.
- Use real coins when teaching money.
- Digital talking watches can be used for teaching time.
- Inlaid geometric puzzles are useful for teaching fractions.
- Use black line graph paper.
- Large print texts or the use of a closed circuit television can be especially helpful in providing enlarged images of charts, diagrams, fractions and when teaching geometry.

Language Arts

- Labelled objects in the room should be at the student's eye level.
- Point out details in pictures to aid with comprehension.
- Use a template or line guide to help a student focus on what they're reading.

- Adjustable reading stands can promote good reading posture and reduce neck and back fatigue.
- Emphasis should be placed on vocabulary building, word-attack skills and comprehension rather than speed. Students with low vision will read slower.
- Large print is not necessary for all students with low vision. Often normal print held close to the eyes is legible. Bold, clear print is best.
- Oral drills will help improve the student's spelling.
- Paper with well-spaced bold black lines is useful for printing and handwriting.
- The younger student should have a written example of the alphabet on his/her own desk.
- The student should be given time to practice reading handwriting.
- Introduce keyboarding skills by grade 3 or 4.

Arts Education

- When written music is used, a larger format and darker staff lines may be necessary.
- Encourage the student to develop an interest in playing an instrument.
- Develop the student's appreciation of music.
- Encourage the student with low vision to attempt the same visual arts activities as other students.
- Paper with raised line drawing or black line drawing will indicate where the student should colour.
- Clay and paper sculpture, textile arts, 3-dimensional forms, finger painting and collage are art forms and activities that students with visual impairments can enjoy.

- Participation in drama provides the opportunity to learn everyday gestures and movements that the student with low vision may not learn through visual observation.
- A heavy string or tape on the floor will indicate where the student should walk and move to on the stage in drama.

Science

- Raised line, large print or bold line diagrams can be used. Avoid detail.
- Assistance may be required in a lab to describe changes and aid in measurement.
- The student should be allowed to examine the apparatus and materials before an experiment. Some science equipment is available with tactile markings.
- The student should be as close as possible to a demonstration.

Social Studies

- Raised line, large print or bold line maps and atlases should be used. Too much detail may be confusing.
- Use large print textbooks.
- Reference materials may be scanned and listened to on a computer with voice access to decrease the amount of reading required.

Industrial Arts

- Orientation of the room should take place before the term begins.
- One-to-one instruction may be needed to teach the student what the tools are and their location.

- The student should become proficient with hand tools before advancing to electric tools. Hand-over-hand instruction may be necessary.
- Students with low vision should be taught to use equipment as if they had no vision. Working in this way will prevent them from holding their faces dangerously close to the equipment

SPECIAL NEEDS OF STUDENTS WITH BLINDNESS

A student with blindness has unique curriculum needs that include:

- concept development;
- organizational skills;
- communication skills (listening, braille reading skills, writing skills, speaking);
- mathematics skills;
- recreation and leisure;
- sexuality education;
- career education;
- self-concept and socialization;
- physical education/sensory motor activities;
- life skills; and
- orientation and mobility.

These unique curriculum areas need to be included in the personal programme plan.

Concept Development

Students with blindness need assistance in making the connection between vocabulary and real objects, body movements and abstract ideas. These students miss incidental learning available to the sighted student and frequently develop inaccurate concepts. The following strategies will aid in concept development.

- Pre-teach vocabulary and key concepts which relate to the curriculum through verbal explanations and concrete experiences using a multi-sensory approach. For example, orient the student to the library before the library time or develop the concept of the skeletal system with real bones.
- Pre-teaching can be provided by someone other than the teacher, such as a peer, an older student, a teacher assistant or a parent.
- After the student has participated in pre-teaching and classroom instruction, it is crucial to review concepts and vocabulary. Say, "Describe what you understand by this term."
- Concepts must be experienced repeatedly in various environments in order for the information to be generalized and for the student to gain expertize.

Organizational Skills

Organizational skills are an integral part of student success and are essential for the student with blindness.

- Have the student organize, use and take responsibility for his/her personal work space.
- Provide the student with a definite place to put things, with the expectation that the student use this space.
- Use containers and zippered pencil cases to store objects.
- Provide a tray for objects that may roll easily off the desk.

Use techniques for safely locating and searching for dropped objects. Attach braille labels to binders and folders for the student. Provide sufficient space for materials and equipment. Often a special room is required for storage and use of specialized equipment. A desk may need to be adapted to provide a larger working area.

Communication Skills

Listening Skills

A student with blindness learns through listening, so it is important that he/she develop good listening skills. Listening skills are taught as an integral part of the language arts curriculum in the elementary grades and a student with blindness will benefit from these activities. In addition, it will be necessary to teach the following skills.

Perceptual awareness and interpretation of environmental sounds:

- discriminate between different sounds;
- locate the direction of sounds; and
- associate sounds with objects and situations.

Listening and interpreting oral information:

- to listen for sequence;
- to listen for details; to listen for main ideas; to listen to follow instructions; and
- new vocabulary. Check that the vocabulary is within the student's experience and has meaning.

Listening to audiocassettes:

- minimize distractions to increase attending;
- read the questions to be answered before listening to the information;

- listen to the pertinent parts of the tape prior to the lesson;
- play a short portion of the tape, then stop to write notes; and
- adjust the speed of the recorder.

Listening to a reader:

Having someone read to the student has the following advantages:

- the student has immediate access to the same reading material as other students;
- the reader can scan the text to find appropriate material; the reader can give information on spelling and punctuation; and this is an option when taking tests.

Braille Reading Skills

The student will require a pre-braille and braille reading programme, in addition to participating in the regular reading programme.

Writing Skills

- Teach a student who uses braille to write his/her signature. Raised lined paper and signature guides are available.
- Teach keyboarding skills (grade 3 or 4) after the braille writing skills are established.
- Provide access to a computer at an early age. Adaptations may be necessary.
- The student should be able to spell words letter by letter as well as by using braille contractions.
- Encourage a student to use the Perkins Brailler as early as pre-school. As braille proficiency increases,

teach the use of a slate and stylus and an electronic braillewriter. Refer to Section VII.

– Options for taking notes are: dictation by the teacher; provision of a print copy to be brailled for the student; scanned by the student and then listened to and/or brailled; tape record the lesson with notes to be brailled later; use of a scribe; braille a peer's notes.

– Check periodically to ensure that the student is making accurate notes.

Speaking Skills

A student should:

- look directly at the speaker;
- learn to participate in a discussion;
- learn when to speak;
- learn to use and interpret voice modulation;
- learn to initiate and contribute to a conversation;
- learn to express thoughts in an organized fashion;
- learn assertiveness skills; and
- develop the ability to ask for and refuse help.

Recreation and Leisure

Recreation and leisure activities will vary with the student's age and functional vision. These activities may range from pretending and playing with toys to artistic abilities and using technology, equipment and tools. Recreation and leisure offer opportunities for students to use their abilities, be active, feel self-worth, release tension, show others what they can do, get along with others and receive recognition or rewards. Many recreation and leisure activities promote lifetime skills that play an important part in developing a satisfactory life. Recreation and leisure activities provide opportunities for students to integrate and apply skills acquired in many curricular areas. Students with blindness need additional encouragement to pursue these activities. The student should develop:

- an awareness of leisure activities and the skills to manage leisure time well;
- skills for solitary play and solitary leisure activities;
- skills for social play and social leisure activities;
- an interest in learning about or joining a community club or group;
- an interest in physical play, physical games, physical fitness and sports;
- an enjoyment of pets and nature;
- an enjoyment of music and dance;
- an interest in a hobby;
- skills for reading, writing, speaking and drama as leisure activities;
- skills for using science and technology for leisure purposes;
- an interest in taking lessons (music, gym, drama, swimming, dance); and
- an interest in attending camps.

Sexuality Education

Sexuality encompasses much more than sex. It is fundamental to our understanding of ourselves and others. It includes topics such as body image, dress, body language, interactions with the same or opposite sex, dating, marriage, intercourse and child bearing. In our society, most sexual information is learned visually. A student with blindness may be unaware or ignorant in this crucial area and may therefore be at high risk for sexual abuse. Parents must be involved in planning and/or teaching sexuality. It is never too early to begin discussing and teaching sexuality with a student who has blindness. The older a child with blindness is before receiving sexuality education, the more difficult it becomes to comprehend the basic concepts. The concepts described in the top of this section and the ones listed below should be taught:

- menstruation, intercourse, conception, pregnancy, menopause;
- sexually transmitted diseases, birth control;
- sexual preferences;
- prevention of sexual abuse;
- privacy;
- genetics;
- dating, social mores, intimate relationships; and
- verbal and non-verbal sexual cues.

Career Education

Unemployment and underemployment of adults with blindness is a continuing concern. Career education is essential to the employability of adults with blindness. A student needs to explore deliberately a wide variety of career options. He/she also needs to develop a realistic understanding of his/her limitations and potential. Emphasize the following:

- self awareness;
- career awareness;
- career exploration (application forms);
- job preparation (interview skills, resume writing, specific training);

— job seeking skills; and
— Employment Assistance for People with Disabilities (EAPD) and other sources of funding.

Self-Concept and Socialization

Blindness will interfere with a student's ability to observe appropriate social behaviours and to learn basic life skills. Social and life skills that other students learn naturally through observing others and modeling, must be taught specifically to the student with blindness.

— Teach the student to turn and face the speaker.
— A student with blindness may have mannerisms, such as rocking or repeatedly rubbing the eyes. Such mannerisms can interfere with social interactions. This is a sensitive issue; professional advice should be sought.
— Encourage the student to initiate a converzation or play activity. The student will often wait silently until someone else takes the initiative.
— Help the student to understand and respect the personal space of others. The student will also need to be able to ask others, in a courteous way, to respect his or her personal space.
— The student with blindness will need to explore objects tactually to gain information and form accurate concepts. However, it is necessary for the student to learn when it is acceptable to touch, particularly when this relates to appropriate and inappropriate physical contact.
— Encourage the student to communicate his/her needs.
— Encourage the student to participate in a variety of group activities.

- Learning nonverbal communication skills is important. Help the student interpret facial expressions, body language and gestures.
- The student needs to learn and demonstrate courteous behaviour.
- Help the student recognize emotions and express them in socially acceptable ways.
- The student will need to learn skills in problem solving and decision making.
- The student needs to develop a positive and accurate self-concept.
- The student should be able to recognize and share feelings about his/her blindness.
- The student needs to become aware of and respond to peer pressure.
- Provide counselling and support for adolescents. This is the stage when students will experience puberty, learn about relationships and dating and need to come to terms with not being able to drive a car. It is particularly important for the student to develop a strong self-image at a time when peer acceptance is influenced by appearance and behaviour.

Physical Education/Sensory Motor Activities

Blindness will diminish the motivation to learn basic motor skills and will also reduce the opportunity to practice these skills. Physical fitness is as important for the student with blindness as the sighted child. Sensory-motor skills are necessary for good concept development, physical conditioning and orientation and mobility skills.

The student with blindness should participate in the regular physical education programme. Adaptations may be required depending on the physical skills of the student. He/She may not be able to participate in all activities and team sports. A parallel or alternate physical activity should be provided.

Daily Living Skills

All children, both sighted and visually impaired, need to learn self-care skills. With blindness, this may take more direct teaching using task analysis. It is important for all children to be able to contribute to the family chores, both for purposes of developing self-esteem and learning to function independently. The student needs the following skills:

- personal hygiene;
- dressing, organization and care of clothing;
- table manners and eating;
- eating-out;
- money management;
- preparing food;
- housekeeping;
- shopping;
- use of the telephone and other communication technology;
- health and safety;
- time concepts;
- self-advocacy;
- problem-solving and decision-making;
- organizing of personal property and time;
- organizing books, materials and equipment;
- develop an understanding of completing tasks on time;

- be able to plan time usage and how to balance time between tasks;
- assume responsibility for materials and equipment;
- use address books, calendars, journals and other personal organization tools;
- be able to follow a time-table; and
- keep track of assignments, grades, schedule changes.

Orientation and Mobility

Children with blindness need to learn techniques that enable safe and efficient travel from an early age if they are to function independently in and be knowledgeable about their environment.

A student needs to understand and be able to tell others comfortably about the cause of his/her blindness. Understanding of the following leads to acceptance and dealing with the blindness:

- name, cause, implications and prognosis of the student's eye condition;
- genetics counseling;
- eye care and service; and
- knowledge of factors secondary to eye condition (diet, medication)

5

SPECIAL EDUCATIONAL NEEDS OF DEAF CHILDREN

Deafness itself does not affect a person's intellectual capacity or ability to learn. Yet, deaf children generally require some form of special intervention and schooling in order to gain an adequate education.

Deaf children have unique communication needs: unable to hear the continuous, repeated flow of language interchange around them, they are not automatically exposed to the enormous amounts of language stimulation experienced by hearing children. For deaf children early, consistant, and continuous use of visible communication modes such as a sign language, finger spelling and cued speech together with amplification and aural/oral training can help reduce the risk of a language delay.

People who are not themselves handicapped tend to group all children with a handicap together—they do not see a blind child or a speech-retarded child, a deaf child or a mentally retarded child, but simply a handicapped child who is different. If the people who take care of a deaf child are not made aware of the specific consequences of being deaf, and if they do not see the child as a child who is normal except for his lack of hearing, they make him different and abnormal simply by treating him so.

Sometimes educational planners do not consider the specific consequences of different handicaps. They take Special Education to mean Education of the Handicapped with no consideration of the differences between the handicaps. But children with different handicaps have very different educational needs, and each group of handicapped children has more in common with non-handicapped children than with other groups of handicapped children.

A deaf child's main problem is to acquire language when he is surrounded by people who use a language that depends on hearing. A blind child has quite different problems: he can hear the language, but he does not always understand its meaning because he cannot see what it refers to. To plan the same kind of Special Education for these children just because they are both handicapped is a gross mistake. It is therefore very important to stress that an individual with any kind of handicap has far more in common with non-handicapped people than with an individual with a different handicap. The main problem for a deaf or severely hard-of-hearing child is to acquire a language in which he can communicate freely and which furthers his intellectual, social, and emotional development.

A deaf individual always feels handicapped when he is in a group of hearing people because he cannot hear what is being said and cannot respond quickly and smoothly. When deaf people meet, they always find that they have common experiences because of their handicap, and they generally feel more at ease with other deaf people because they can communicate with them on equal terms. However, most deaf children have hearing parents and siblings, and all deaf people live in societies dominated by hearing people.

Deaf children therefore need to develop a double identity: as members of deaf people's community and as members of the society at large. To make such a development possible, they should be offered contact both with deaf children and deaf adults using a sign language and with hearing people.

Educational planners and teachers should carefully consider what it means not to be able to acquire the language used by hearing people spontaneously, but they should also see deaf children as individuals with all the same potentials for intellectual, physical, social, cultural, and emotional development as other children.

The main goal of educating deaf children is to give them the same possibilities of participating in the society in adult life as other people have. Integration is a key word in all work with not only deaf people, but all handicapped people. However, because of the special communicative consequences of deafness, deaf people seriously risk being isolated if they are integrated with hearing people without any contact with other deaf people. On the surface it may look like integration, but a deaf individual has no chance of real participation if he is only surrounded by hearing and speaking people. This situation increases his handicap.

Real participation can only be obtained on deaf people's own terms. That is, they should be offered possibilities of being together with other deaf people, and they should take part in making decisions about their own lives. Only by acquiring self-confidence in this way, will they also be able to participate in the hearing society.

In order to reach this aim, it is necessary to establish pre-school programmes, schools, or sections in schools especially for deaf children. If the society invests in giving special training in deaf education to some teachers, their expertise is used to more advantage if deaf children are gathered in special schools rather than being integrated in normal programmes individually. Consideration should also be given to establishing prevocational and vocational training to meet deaf people's communication needs.

CAUSES OF DEAFNESS

Most parents want to know why their child is deaf. The causes of deafness can be categorized as follows:

1. acquired deafness
2. hereditary (genetic) deafness
3. unidentified reasons.

Acquired deafness covers approximately half of the cases, and the causes can be divided into several subgroups:

(a) injury at birth

(b) infection in the pregnant mother such as rubella or cytomegalovirus infection or toxoplasmosis

(c) infection in the child such as meningitis, measles, mumps, or severe infections of the middle ear

(d) the use of drugs.

Several antibiotics have been found to cause deafness if the mother takes them during pregnancy or if they are given to the infant. These drugs have the same effect no matter whether they are taken by injection or by mouth. They should therefore not be given to pregnant women and small children unless their lives are in danger.

Some cases of *genetic deafness* develop after birth, and a few cases become more severe as the child grows older. In order to diagnose whether deafness is caused by heredity, it is necessary to examine the family and its health history. Sometimes there is no evidence of deafness in the family, but the cause can be still hereditary. It may then be a recessive inheritance, where the parents have normal hearing, but are carriers of an abnormal gene which may develop deafness in the offspring.

The unidentified causes of deafness cover approximately 25 per cent of all cases—and it should be stressed that causes of deafness are very difficult to determine.

When the parents have just been told that their child is deaf, they are usually too shocked to understand information about the possible causes of their child's deafness. If you suspect that the cause is hereditary, the parents should be given advice and information before planning to have other children. However, in other cases, information should be given little by little at a rate at which the parents can understand and tolerate it.

EDUCATING THE DEAF PRE-SCHOOL CHILD

Early Detection in Collaboration with Parents

Early detection, diagnosis, and treatment are important to give the deaf child optimal conditions for development.

When a child does not respond to loud noises and there is a failure of speech development, one is likely to conclude that something is wrong. But most deaf infants are almost as alert and responsive to their families as normally hearing children, using their visual sense and their senses of feeling and touching to compensate for their lack of hearing. This means that the parents do not discover the hearing problem. Even when professionals test deaf babies, they may not see that the child is deaf, because he uses his other senses and produces behavioural responses to noise similar to the behaviour of hearing children.

Difficulties in discovering and testing the hearing ability in infants and children may be the main reasons for a delayed detection of a severe hearing loss. Even in countries where early detection and treatment are well organized, deafness is sometimes not discovered until the child's third or fourth year of age.

It is difficult to live with a deaf child day by day, knowing that something is wrong, but not knowing what the implications are or what to do about it. Diagnosis without treatment is cruel, so facilities for early detection and diagnosis should always be accompanied by facilities for parent guidance with positive demonstrations of what parents can do for their child. Every effort should be made to reduce the period between detection and confirmation of irreversible hearing loss and the initiation of an appropriate intervention programme.

Early Intervention and Pre-school Programmes

By early intervention and pre-school programmes we mean programmes for children prior to their entrance in school, that is, children approximately below the age of 6 years.

For the deaf children the programmes should provide:

- possibilities for social, intellectual, and linguistic development based mainly on visual communication
- social contact with other deaf children and deaf adults
- auditory testing and training.

Moreover, the programmes should include advice to the parents concerning:

- information on how to meet the child's basic needs for visual and emotional contact through seeing what goes on around him; he should not be left alone

- information on all possible means of communication with their children: natural gestures, sounds, plays, words spoken near the child's ear, a sign language, cued speech, and finger-spelling
- information on hearing aids: fitting, maintenance, and training in use
- meeting other parents through parents' associations, etc.

More than 90 per cent of all deaf children are born into hearing families with no previous knowledge of deafness. Parents will always remember what they are first told about their child's deafness. It is therefore important that the teachers in the intervention programme be made sensitive to the special needs and abilities of each family. They should avoid a standard approach to giving advice to parents. Moreover, they should always look at the potentials of each family and stress a positive attitude to the child's development.

Parents usually ask, 'Will my child talk?'. Since it is always difficult to tell how a deaf child will develop spoken language, teachers in the intervention programme should always be cautious about giving a definite answer to this question, and they should instead focus on what can be done in the immediate future.

Parents should be informed that their child can develop normally in all areas except spoken language communication. They should be told what they can do to respond to their child's modified communication abilities. The child can learn to communicate, but the means of communication must be adapted to the visual sense. The parents should be informed about the different means of visual communication and of manual aids to spoken language. It is very important that they are offered practical demonstrations of these means so that they are in a position to make a real choice of how to communicate with their child.

Furthermore, they should be encouraged to interact with their child through a natural parent-child relationship. In an attempt to do what they think is best for their child, some parents start teaching their child language and forget to attend to the child's needs for a spontaneous communication. If the parents are not told about the total communication approach and sign language, they have severe problems communicating with their child later in life.

Parents should be encouraged to look for other deaf children and for deaf adults in their local community in order to give their child opportunities of making contact with other deaf individuals. Through contact with other families with deaf members, the parents can exchange experiences and get social and emotional support.

To make pre-school programmes as successful as possible, teachers should tell the parents about what happens to their child in the programme. A close connection between the pre-school programme and the deaf child's family is important in order to create a world in which the family's emotional resources are combined with the school's education of the child.

Any pre-school and early intervention programme should be organized around the children's needs making sure that they are not just being supervized, but are stimulated through plays and spontaneous communication by means of sign language and spoken language. At this age deaf children are open to all ways of communicating, including mime and sign language.

If a deaf child has never before been exposed to mime or sign language, he may be passive and withdrawn. After a .short time in the programme the new visual means of communication may cause a radical change in his behaviour. He starts to communicate with other children and adults and develops language.

Children benefit from participating in early intervention programmes even if it means that they have to be separated from their parents most of the day or even for weeks at a time. They

- develop skills to actively master their world
- develop consideration and special attention to others
- learn to cooperate and communicate with other deaf children
- get opportunities of enjoying playing, being told stories, looking at pictures, and dramatizing
- develop physically through dancing and rhythmic activities
- acquire visual language.

EDUCATING THE DEAF SCHOOL CHILD

As he grows up, a small child learns to speak and understand the language that is spoken by the people around him. But before he starts school, he learns much more than that. He sees people work, eat, sleep, dance, play music, tell stories. He takes part in all these activities, and he hears people talk about what they do and why they do it. He sees people die, children being born, and young people marrying. He sees how these events are celebrated, and again he hears people talk about why they happen.

Little by little the child learns not only a language, but also a way of life, sets of values, and common knowledge about life and death, the change of the seasons, and much more. The acquisition of a language cannot be separated from the acquisition of ways of perceiving what we do and why we do it, how we interact with other people, and the values we attach to our actions and what goes on around us.

A deaf child can see the same things as a hearing child, but if he lives isolated among people who cannot communicate with him, he does not hear how people talk about what happens around them and why they do what they do. When such a child comes to the school for the deaf, he has no language, but, just as importantly, he does not have the knowledge about what goes on around him that we normally expect a child to have acquired in infancy. He only knows as much about how to interact with other people as he has been able to infer from looking at others, he knows little about people's motives for acting and he does not share the values that are taken for granted in his society.

It is first and foremost the teacher's task to give the child the knowledge and values that are essential to being a member of his society. In doing this, the teacher should use any means of communication that the child understands and that will give him a tool for analyzing and expressing his thoughts, hopes, and fears about his life and the world that he lives in. Acquiring language and acquiring world knowledge go hand in hand. Language learning cannot be separated from the children's increasing knowledge about the world around them from their daily experiences, and in teaching the children about this world in subjects like geography, mathematics, and health care, teachers also teach them language.

The languages that the teachers can use with deaf children are a sign language and a vocal language in its spoken and written form. Unless their families or other people around them have signed to them before they came to the school, deaf children do not know a sign language when they start school. Teachers therefore cannot expect the children to understand them just because they sign. But deaf children can acquire a sign language by seeing people use it. They do not need systematic training in signing. By contrast, deaf children need systematic training in order to acquire a vocal language. Such training should always be combined with the teaching of the knowledge and the sets of values that we want children to acquire. If the children do not understand what goes on around them, systematic training of a vocal language is useless. The teacher should always make sure that the children understand what she conveys and why they should learn a vocal language.

Knowing a Language

Deaf children who start school cannot be expected to know much of the vocal language that they are going to learn to articulate, speech read, read, and write.

When we know a language, we understand what is conveyed in the language and we can use it to tell others what we want them to know. Some people also learn to read and perhaps compose written texts in the language. These four skills can be presented as follows:

	Perception	*Production*
Spoken language	Understand by hearing	Speak meaningfully
Written language	Read with understanding	Compose in writing

Behind all four skills is a knowledge of the language that we do not normally separate from the skills, but we can of course hear a language without understanding it, and we can imitate a sentence that is spoken in a language we do not know. We would not call that speaking the language, as we presuppose understanding in our conception of what it is to speak a language. We cannot speak a language unless we understand what we are saying.

Different Levels

Children are not alike, and teachers should always expect them to reach different levels in any skill. Some deaf children may get very far in speaking a vocal language, perhaps because they are good at using their residual hearing. Others find it much harder to learn to articulate the language even with considerable residual hearing. We do not know the reasons for this difference.

We know, however, that there is some correlation between the levels reached in speechreading, reading, and writing. The reason for this correlation is that these skills depend heavily on how well a person knows the language. If you know a language well, it is much easier to speechread.

It is extremely difficult to learn to speechread a language you cannot hear and to articulate this language when you do not get any feedback from your own voice. It may cause deep frustration if teachers spend much time on teaching deaf children a vocal language mainly in its spoken form. We are so used to seeing the skills of speaking and understanding spoken language as prerequisites of reading and writing that we find it hard to understand that it is possible to learn a language merely in its written form. This is possible, however, and as it is so important that deaf children are given a tool to communicate with the hearing people of their society, it is advisable to give priority to the skills of reading and writing in teaching deaf children. Some children advance faster and become more skilled than other children. Teachers should not force the children who are less advanced, but always make the most of what each child knows to push him a little forward.

Starting to Teach a Deaf Child

When a deaf child starts school, the teacher should make

sure that he gets as much information as possible about the child, his family, and his local town or village. To this end it is useful to make out an inquiry form that the teacher can use to interview the child's parents or the person who brings the child to the school. It is preferable that the teacher who is going to have the most contact with the child makes the inquiry, as it is very important that this teacher gets as thorough an impression of the child's life before school as possible. If she does not speak the same language as the child's parents, she should make use of an interpreter, for example another teacher at the school who speaks the language.

Contact with the Parents

Most parents wish to see their child grow up, but they may feel that once their child joins a school for deaf children and perhaps even goes away to a residential school, others take over responsibility for him. The parents may even hesitate to visit or write to the child for fear of interfering. It is very important that the teacher makes the parents understand that they are still responsible for their child and that they should take an interest in his upbringing. If the child is sent to the school without his parents coming too, the teacher should write to them and ask them to come to the school.

On their first visit to the school, the teacher should show the parents around so that they become acquainted with the place where their child is going to spend so much time. The teacher should also tell them about her plans for teaching the child. All this makes it easier for the parents to communicate with their child and it makes them feel that they are still responsible for him. The teacher should also invite the parents to come to the school as often as possible, and she should encourage them to write to the child regularly and make it possible for the child to go home during school vacations. It is also to be recommended that the teacher write to the parents regularly and tell them what happens at the school.

Observations

During the child's first months at the school, the teacher should make observations on his health and behaviour.

If the child suffers from infections or other diseases, he cannot be expected to have sufficient energy to benefit from the teaching. The child's sight should be checked, as he may not be able to follow what the teacher communicates unless he is provided with glasses.

The child's ears should also be examined, if possible by means of an otoscope. If the child's ear drums are ruptured, there is a serious risk of infection, and the child should not be allowed to swim and should be warned against putting anything into his ears. His hearing should be evaluated: Can he identify single words?.

All precautions that are taken as a consequence of the observations on the child's health should be explained to him and to his parents. Here the teacher may find simple line drawings, for example of the ear, helpful.

The teacher should also make observations on the child's way of communicating. Children's level and means of communication may vary considerably. Children from deaf families may be expected to communicate at quite an advanced level of signing, and children whose hearing parents have received guidance about how to communicate with their deaf child may be very attentive to the teacher's communication. But with children who have been isolated in hearing families with no knowledge about the special communicative needs of deaf people, the teacher may find it difficult even to establish eye contact, and without eye contact communication with deaf children is excluded.

To evaluate a child's level and means of communication, the teacher should therefore start by observing if it is difficult to establish eye contact with the child. Moreover, does the child interact with adults or other children on his own initiative, or only when they address him? Does he communicate by means of gestures, pointing, signs, words with or without sound, or merely inarticulate screaming? If the child uses signs, they may be signs that the teacher does not know, either because they have been invented by the child and his family, or because they are only used in the area where the child comes from. The teacher should be very careful not to ignore such signs as they may be a valuable way of making contact with the child. When the teacher makes out what these signs mean, she may gradually show the child the signs that are used at the school instead.

In trying to make out the child's means and level of communication, the teacher may use pictures of people, things, and simple daily situations that the child knows and encourage the child to tell what he sees any way he can. But as many children are not used to seeing pictures, the teacher should also make observations of the child in daily life at the school and make notes of them.

Such observations tell the teacher something about the child's previous experience with language and communication and the level at which she can start teaching. However, the teacher should always be very cautious about drawing conclusions about a child's level of functioning. It may take months or even years before she can form a precise opinion about a child's hearing level or means of communication. The child may feel insecure at the school for a long time, and this influences his performance level both in hearing tests and in communication.

Senior pupils may be a great help in making a new child feel comfortable and open to the new surroundings, and it is a good idea to appoint a senior pupil 'brother" or 'sister" of a new child. He should be told about his obligations to the new child and he should be present when the child comes to the school and during the interview with the child's parents. Children always imitate older children in both their behaviour and their language, and you may see that young deaf children learn to sign from their older friends. They may even invent signs that the teacher does not know, but this should not be prevented as it is part of their becoming members of the pupils' community at the school.

Arrangement of the School and the Classroom

The arrangement of schools for deaf children should be adapted to the children's special needs.

As deaf children are generally less aware of what goes on in the local community and in the world at large, it is useful to put up lots of pictures on the walls. A couple of cameras should be given high piority when the school is provided with technical equipment. A camera permits you to put up single photos of all the pupils and the staff from the headmaster to the janitor with their names written underneath each photo. This is one way of making deaf children understand what it means to have a name. You can also take photos of things that the children see on excursions from the school, and of important events like celebrations at the school. Such photos make it much easier to discuss with the children what they have seen.

Maps of their country, photos from their home towns or villages, and pictures of foreign countries and their people are also useful to enlarge the children's knowledge. Such pictures may not be easy to get hold of, but any pictures' will do—photos from newspapers and magazines and drawings made by the teacher and the pupils.

The classrooms should be arranged in such a way that all the children can see both the teacher and each other, as deaf children can only communicate with others when they have eye contact with them. This means that there should not be more than 10 pupils per class. To facilitate speechreading the teacher should sit at a low chair so that her face is at the same level as the children's faces. Moreover, there should be strong light on both the pupils and the teacher, which makes it preferable that the windows are not behind either the teacher or the children.

When the children work in smaller groups, the tables can be arranged in groups that facilitate communication between the children.

The classrooms should be provided with notice boards for putting up pictures and texts, and with a blackboard and a flip-over. An overhead projector is a great help in showing texts and drawings that the teacher has prepared in advance, but it depends on electricity, and a flip-over may serve the same functions.

With hearing children you can easily tell them something about a picture in their textbooks while each child looks at the picture in his own book, because hearing children can listen to the teacher without looking at her, but deaf children can only understand what the teacher tells them if they look at her. All the children should therefore look at the same text or the same picture so that the teacher can point at words or passages in the text or details of the picture while she explains them. As soon as the children look down in their books, all communication with the teacher stops. A blackboard and a flip-over are therefore even more important in a school for deaf children than in a school for hearing children.

If the school can provide the children with hearing aids, the rooms should be equipped in such a way that noise is absorbed, as a hearing aid in a room with a stone floor and a roof of corrugated iron is worthless. Pictures, drawings, and notice boards of cloth on the walls improve the acoustics of the rooms.

Communication Strategies in the Classroom

To accord communication in the classroom the best possible conditions, the teacher should observe the following:

(a) There should be strong lighting all over the room.

(b) Never speak to the children if they do not look at you.

(c) Always speak or sign turned directly towards the children, and not with your back or side towards them (e.g. when writing on the blackboard). When you use spoken language, always speak with a normal rhythm and intonation.

(d) Use all kinds of clues to visualize what you are talking about: pointing, drawings, pictures, key-words on the blackboard, dramatizing.

(e) Always make the children aware of who is communicating at the moment, also when other children sign or speak. Otherwise the communication turns into a dialogue between the teacher and only one child at a time.

(f) Be prepared to repeat comments, questions, and answers from the children so that everyone can benefit from what goes on. Even when an answer is unexpected or different from the answer that you want, you should repeat it if you see that somebody has missed it.

(g) Make the children discuss subjects and problems brought up among the children, even if you do not fully understand their sign language. It is of the

uttermost importance that they get the opportunity of learning language from each other.

Teaching Methods

Activities to develop language and world knowledge

As deaf children often lack much knowledge and many skills that we expect of children of the same age, the teacher should put much weight on activities that integrate language learning, acquiring practical skills, and acquiring knowledge of the society in which the children live. Especially at the lower level, the children's day should not be split into subjects like mathematics, reading, geography, etc., but these subjects should be integrated in activities like playing, excursions, and story telling. The children may start learning basic arithmetical skills like numbers and simple counting by buying foodstuff at a market or paying the fare in a bus with the teacher's assistance, and they may learn about different occupations from visiting workshops, offices, etc. Botany learnt by seeing how plants are grown is of more use to the children than botany learnt from a book.

During the first months in a new class, the main activities should be various kinds of plays that permit the teacher to make observations on the children's communication and behaviour. Many children are not used to using a pencil or a pair of scissors, playing with things like dolls and toy cars, or looking at pictures. The teacher should initiate plays where she takes on various roles like playing a mother taking care of her baby or selling foodstuff at a market, or a grandfather taking his grandchild to school for the first time. These plays imitate real situations from the children's lives.

In the plays the teacher and the children may use toys (dolls, toy cars, small toy chairs, etc.) and things from daily life (dishes, bags, bottles, etc.). If toys cannot be provided, the teacher should use her imagination to make things out of what is available.

In the beginning the children may not understand what is expected of them. Then the teacher must act several roles and gradually try to draw the children into the plays. She should make clear to them that the plays follow certain rules. For example, you cannot buy something at a market just by taking it, you must pay for it and you must await your turn, and you cannot leave a child (a doll) just anywhere, but should make sure that he is safe. In regulating the play, the teacher should encourage the children to follow certain rules and make them confident in taking part.

It is very important to develop the children's sense of time. This can be done by beginning every day by discussing with the children what they did the day before, what they are going to do that day, and what they will do the following day. To visualize this, the teacher should draw a calendar of the three days.

The various activities may be illustrated by means of drawings and, in higher grades, described in words. The children should also get a sense of greater spans of time, the days of the week and the months of the year according to the calendar of the culture in which they live. Here the teacher should use two more calendars.

In the calendar of the week you indicate the activities of the current week. In the calendar of the year you fasten pictures and drawings and illustrate festivals and typical activities of each month, and you indicate the current month as well as events of special interest to the children such as vacations. Such calendars should be used through all grades as they make the children more confident about what is happening around them, but you should not spend more than 10-15 minutes per day on this topic.

The teacher should also take the children on excursions outside the school. They may visit markets, construction sites, workshops, farms, etc., take part in festivals and celebrations, or collect insects, plants, shells, or stones. The point is that the children experience as much of the normal life around them as possible. They may integrate these experiences in their plays, enacting situations from the market or the workshop in the classroom.

But the children's experiences from playing and excursions must not be left at that. The teacher should make drawings of things or situations from the plays or the excursions, and she should encourage the children to do the same. Teachers should not let their lack of skill in drawing prevent them from making simple drawings. With a little training anyone can make simple line drawings of people and the most common things around them.

The teacher should communicate with the children about what they see and explain why people do what they do and why they follow certain rules in their interaction with each other. To this end she may use signs, pantomime, spoken language, and drawings in any combination that makes the children understand her.

It is helpful to have an adult deaf assistant in the class both in play situations and on excursions as a deaf adult may know better how to visualize things and situations in explaining them to the children. If there are not the resources for an assistant, it may be a good idea to unite two classes for some activities like excursions or playing so that there may be two adults with the group.

Stories should be an important part of the teaching through all grades. It is very helpful in developing the children's skills in signing that a deaf adult tells them stories in sign language, but the teacher may also use any means of communication—signing, spoken language, pantomime, and drawings—that makes the children understand.

Even though the children cannot read, they should get used to identifying texts and the functions that writing may have. The teacher should therefore put up pictures with texts from newspapers and magazines. Wrappings from goods and foodstuff with texts written on them may be integrated in the playing. The teacher should not expect the children to read these texts. At appropriate moments she should explain that the texts tell what is inside the wrappings or they describe what you see on the pictures.

The activities during the first period make the children understand what it means to communicate and to take part in rule-governed interaction between people. They also learn the difference between an object and a representation of the object like a toy or a drawing, and they begin to understand why people do what they do. All this is essential to learning language. Moreover, the children learn social behaviour like buying goods at a market and going by bus, and practical skills like using a pencil, a pair of scissors, a needle, etc.

Children who prefer to use their left hand in handling a pencil or a needle, should not be forced to use their right hand as this may hamper them considerably, and they can become as skilled in writing with their left hand as others are in writing with their right hand.

The first subjects

Very early the teacher should make the children understand that they have names. She can do this by drawing the outline of each child on the blackboard, on large sheets of paper or in the sand. Then she says each child's name, finger-spells it and writes it within the drawing of the child's outline. Some children have name signs which the teacher should add to the vocalizations of their names.

When writing and finger-spelling the children's names, the teacher should not worry about whether the children know each single letter at this early stage. Exposure to writing and finger-spelling is an important first step in understanding what writing is. Little-by-little the children learn to recognize some whole words and sentences in writing, and not until later should they learn to break the words down into letters.

The period spent on making the children understand what a name is may vary very much from one group of children to another, but it may easily last several weeks. Of course, during this period teaching the children their names should be mixed with other activities like excursions, playing, physical training, storytelling, etc.

When the children have learnt what a name is, they should learn about the difference between being a boy and a girl. They should realize that some of them are boys and some of them girls, and that some of the teachers are men and some women. Here the teacher may use play situations to demonstrate the different duties and rights of boys and girls and men and women, but she should also make the children understand that some activities are common to both sexes. Both men and women can be teachers, for instance.

Now the teacher adds the sentence '(Name) is a boy' or '(Name) is a girl' to the photos or drawings of the children, and she may also choose to add sentences describing a few typical activities of boys and girls or men and women. In doing so, she should always make sure that the children understand what is meant by the written sentences, and she should be very cautious not to introduce too many new words at a time. To make sure that the children understand the sentence, she should encourage them to make drawings that illustrate their meanings, and ask them to write the sentences underneath the drawings. The children may also dramatize the meaning of the sentences to demonstrate their understanding.

Deafness as a topic

When the children feel confident about being at school and see themselves as members of a group of deaf children, the teacher should begin to make clear to them what deafness is, what sound is, and what the difference between deaf and hearing people is. Hearing people can understand each other even when they have their backs turned. You can demonstrate this by asking a child to hand something of his own choice to you. Then you tell what it is to a hearing person with his back turned. He can then tell what the child handed to you - without magic! But hearing people cannot communicate through a glass window as you can when you sign, and they may find it difficult to communicate in noisy localities. Moreover, they may be greatly bothered by noise.

The children should also be told that hearing children learn to speak and understand a vocal language without training when they are quite small, but that they do make mistakes. It may comfort and amuse deaf children to be told some of these mistakes when they themselves have problems learning a vocal language.

It is very important that the children understand the consequences of being deaf - that they will not acquire hearing as they grow up, and that their choice of occupation is limited due to their handicap. In this process deaf adults may be very helpful as they can better explain to the children what it is like to be deaf, and as they can serve as models of adults with whom the children can identify.

Little-by-little it should also be made clear to the children why it is useful to learn a vocal language. If deaf children go to residential schools and are never taken outside the school, they do not get a realistic view of how one manages to live in a hearing society as a deaf person. The children should therefore be encouraged to interact as much as possible with the surrounding society, for instance by buying things for the school. Such situations demonstrate the need for good skills in the vocal language.

The teacher should discuss these topics with the children when she sees that they are preoccupied with deafness and their future choice of vocational training, but she should also make sure that the topics are part of the curriculum.

Teaching reading and writing

Reading and writing should be integrated with other subjects and activities such as playing, excursions, and story telling. It is important to start with an experience that the children have in common, like a visit to the local mill, as this permits the teacher to make sure that the children understand what she writes on the flip-over or the blackboard.

Stories are another excellent source for reading and writing. All children love to be told stories, and the first purpose of telling a story is to make them experience the thrill and pleasure of a good story. Once the teacher has made sure that the children understand the story, for instance by making them draw various situations from the story, she should write a simple version of the story on the flip-over and go through the text with the children. Here she explains the meaning of words and phrases and points to their representation in writing. In such situations a flip-over is very helpful as it permits the teacher to write the story in advance. She may illustrate it either in advance or while telling it, which gives her a possibility of checking the children's understanding. The use of the flip-over allows the teacher to preserve the story for use in subsequent lessons.

From experiences that the children have in common the teacher may go on to the children's individual experiences. She encourages them to tell about their own experiences in the schoolyard or at home and then she writes what they tell in simple sentences like '(Name) tells: "Yesterday I saw a truck".' But the teacher should encourage the children to tell their experiences in such a way that all the children in the classroom understand them.

When the teacher has written a sentence on the blackboard or the flip-over, she should explain what it means, read it aloud and ask the children to read it aloud and explain in signs, pantomime, or drawings what it means.

When the children have learned to recognize some sentences and words, the teacher can start breaking down the words into letters and make the children see how the letters are repeated in other words and how they are articulated. She should encourage the children to speechread simple words that she articulates, imitate her articulation and write the words by means of the letters that they know. Finger-spelling is very helpful in teaching the children to write.

In order to introduce new words the teacher may make drawings of their meanings on cards and write the words on other cards. When she has explained the meaning of a new word to the children, she encourages them to articulate it and to match the word card with the card with the drawing.

Special material that demonstrates the ideal progression in language training of deaf children is available in very few languages. Adults usually know more or less intuitively how to speak to small children - they use simple sentences and common words. In choosing sentences to present to deaf children, teachers should therefore trust their intuitions about which sentences are simple and which are difficult because of their complexity, and they should expose the children to the sentences in this order.

Once the children get more used to writing, teachers should, however, not hesitate to show them complex sentences that the children cannot construct themselves. They may need some help from the teacher in order to understand such sentences, but we should expect deaf children to become more advanced in reading than in composing.

As deaf children do not know the language of the textbooks and often do not have the same knowledge as hearing children of the same age, textbooks are of little use in the beginning. During the first couple of years the teacher should only use ordinary textbooks as a source of providing illustrations and stories that she can tell the children. Gradually the textbooks may be integrated in the teaching as the children's knowledge of the language and writing increases, but the teacher should go on checking that the children understand what they read. Here she should not hesitate to ask even children in higher grades to make drawings of what they understand.

The teacher should distinguish between two kinds of reading. One is reading for pleasure: the children should be encouraged to make out as much as possible of the content of a text without paying attention to details of the language. The other one is close reading: the teacher explains difficult words, phrases, and sentence constructions.

The same distinction can be made in composition. If the children write something spontaneously, for instance on a drawing, the teacher should not correct errors unless the child asks for the correct spelling of a word. In situations where the children have been asked to write something, the teacher may insist on correctness. However, she should never expect full correctness of deaf children, as it is very difficult to learn to compose in a language that one cannot hear.

Sex guidance

Subjects that are very important at all levels are health care, sanitation, and sex guidance. Many teachers find sex guidance very difficult, both because the children's parents may be opposed to it and because the teachers themselves feel restrained by their own modesty. Many hearing children receive traditional sex guidance according to the culture they belong to, and they often overhear more or less concealed references to sex made by older children and adults.

Deaf children cannot benefit from traditional sex guidance or from occasional references to sex as they do not understand what is being said. Deaf children have a right to be told about this very important side of life and a right to information that permits them to take care of themselves.

Curriculum and Materials

The main difference between deaf and hearing children is the way they are taught rather than the subjects they are taught. Teachers should therefore be prepared to follow the ordinary curriculum for hearing children, but with some delay compared with these children and using other methods. Because of their handicap deaf children need some supplementary subjects like what deafness is, what it is like to hear, and what you can accomplish in spite of a hearing handicap. Moreover, deaf children need to be told more explicitly about feelings, motives, attitudes, beliefs, and accepted ways of interacting with other people, and their handicap implies that we cannot expect them to reach the same level in vocal language skills as hearing children. They also need special training in articulation and speechreading and training of their residual hearing.

It can be recommended that teachers make individual plans of how they want to teach a specific class. Here they should make clear to themselves which topics they want to teach and in which order. Moreover, they should make clear how and when they want to expose the children to written language and which constructions and words they want to teach the children. They should also consider how they want to integrate playing and excursions outside the school, and which materials like pictures, films, toys, books, and stories they have at their disposition, and how they should be integrated in the teaching.

Teachers should expect to use textbooks published for use in schools for hearing children with some dealy, and they should find it natural to use other kinds of texts and pictures in the teaching. Old newspapers and magazines, books for children and adults, wrappings from foodstuffs and other products may all fulfil the need for written material that exposes the children to written language and its functions. All kinds of toys, miniature objects, tools, and natural objects like stones, fruits, and plants should be taken into the classroom for playing with and for illustrating the content of texts. In order to give deaf children an impression of the values and beliefs passed on between generations, the teacher should also integrate myths and stories in a form that the deaf children of her class can understand.

TRAINING VOCAL SKILLS

Training Residual Hearing

Hearing losses affect people's hearing in very different ways. Some children can only hear loud sounds, some can only hear high notes, and some only low notes. In training the children's residual hearing, teachers should, therefore, pay attention to both volume and pitch.

In the beginning the main purpose of training a child's residual hearing is to make the child interested in sounds and train his ability to discern sound from silence. To do so you may give the child a ball or a small bag with dried peas and tell him to throw the bag into a bowl in front of him when he hears a sound. Then you place yourself behind the child with a drum or two lids and when you make a sound, the child should throw the ball or bag.

Children who are profoundly deaf can get an impression of the difference between sound and silence by touching an instrument like a drum or a guitar when it vibrates and when it is silent. Indicate by pointing to your ears and by an attentive facial expression that you can perceive the sound without touching the instrument. You can also make the child touch your throat so that he feels the vibrations when you speak.

Children who can hear the difference between sound and silence, should go on to learning to discern the difference between different kinds of sounds—a drum, a guitar, a marimba, lids, a bell, a flute, a voice. The child should play with the instruments and try to make them sound before you train his ability to discern the different sounds. Then the child makes drawings of the instruments, and you explain to him that when you make a sound behind his back, he should point to the corresponding drawing. You may instead ask him to turn around and point to the instrument.

The next step is training the child's sense of rhythm. This can be done by making the child touch the skin of a drum while you beat a special rhythm. Then you ask him to imitate the rhythm by clapping his hands. Dancing to the rhythms of a drum is another possibility.

If the child seems to profit from the training, you can go on to different animal sounds and different sounds of your own voice. It is to be recommended that you start by training him to discern different vowels. Children with some residual hearing can be trained to discern different words and sentences that you speak close to their ears.

Teaching Speechreading

Speechreading means perceiving speech by looking at the person who speaks. The main source of information to speechreading is the movement of the lips, but as you can see from looking at yourself speaking in a mirror, you cannot discern many sounds by the movements of the lips. If you want to find out how difficult it is, try to speak to your family without using your voice and see if they can understand you.

In speechreading you also draw information from other sources: the movements of the cheeks and the chin, the speaker's facial expression, eye movements, body rhythm, and gestures, your knowledge of the situation in which the communication takes place, and your knowledge of the language.

When we speak, our facial expression reflects our emotions. We usually look happy when we tell that we are pleased with something, or angry when we scold people. When we talk about a thing or a person that we can see from where we stand, we look in the direction of this thing or person. Our body moves in a rhythm that corresponds to the phrases in our speech, and our gestures underline boundaries and stressed words. Some people even use gestures that are vey close to signs in a sign language, and in all cultures there are certain standard gestures used by hearing people like movements of the head for affirmation or denial, pointing, greetings, insulting movements of the hands, etc.

Moreover, in speechreading—and in all language understanding—people draw on their knowledge of the situation and of the people who take part in the communication: What can you expect these people to say in this situation?

The final source of information is our knowledge of the language that is spoken. You can appreciate the importance of this knowledge for speechreading by asking someone to remove every sixth word in a text, for instance a newspaper article, and then you read the text. You will experience that you have no or very little difficulty reading the text. The reason is that you fill in the missing parts on the basis of your knowledge of the language and the topic of the text.

When you teach speechreading to deaf children, you should make sure that the child can draw on as many of the sources of information as possible. Moreover, it is important that there is strong light on your face and that the child has normal sight or is provided with glasses.

In the beginning you must expect the child to know very little of the language. You should therefore use utterances in natural situations where you refer to things in the immediate context, and you should let your facial expression correspond to the emotional content of your utterances.

In special training sessions you may for instance talk about a drawing a child has made, pointing to things in the drawing, telling what they are and expressing your emotions at seeing them. But you should also use other situations as an opportunity to teach speechreading. The routine activities of the class like greetings in the morning, taking out paper and pencils, and cleaning the blackboard, are ideal for such occasional training once you are sure the children know these routines.

The children should be encouraged to guess at the meaning of your utterances on the basis of the clues they can discern, as good guessing is a fundamental part of understanding language.

You can test their understanding by asking them to do things and see if they do as they are asked, or you can ask them to explain by signs or mime what you said. You can also encourage them to repeat what you say, but you should remember that even though a child can repeat more or less accurately what you say, this is no guarantee that he understands the utterance.

Gradually, as the children's knowledge of the vocal language increases, you may go on to more complex sentences and to speaking of absent things and events. When the children become more advanced in speechreading, they should be encouraged to use their ability in communicating with people outside the school.

All the time you should make sure that the children understand why they receive training in speechreading. If they cannot see the importance of being able to interact with hearing people, they cannot be expected to be prepared to spend much energy on trying to learn to speechread. It is therefore essential that the children become as much aware of life outside the school as possible.

As with training residual hearing and speech, you should expect the children to reach different levels. If a child has some residual hearing, he may be able to make good use of it in speechreading, but it depends very much on the nature of his hearing loss.

Speech Training

Deaf children do not develop the spoken language of their community in the same way as normally hearing children do. Due to their lack of hearing they learn neither to understand the spoken language nor to distinguish the different sounds of which language consists. They cannot reproduce sounds correctly as they do not hear them or only hear some of them, and what they hear may even be distorted. Furthermore, they cannot hear their own voice and that is essential to controlling speech.

Depending on the extent of the hearing loss, deaf children may produce some more or less understandable sounds, but they are far behind hearing children in speech development.

For a deaf child it is really hard work and endless struggle to develop speech, and unfortunately the result of years of training does not always meet up with the expectation of the child himself, the parents, and the teacher. Only a small percentage of the children with a great hearing loss achieve intelligible spoken communication skills. Many of them are only able to make themselves understood by their teacher and close family.

All children, hearing as well as deaf, babble, but while hearing children continue to babble until they start forming intelligible sounds and words, the deaf child eventually stops babbling because he does not get any feedback. The hearing child keeps getting feedback from his own voice and from the people around him. All these sounds inspire him to go on experimenting with soundmaking, whereas the deaf child loses interest in producing sound.

If parents have any means of comparison either with older children of their own or children of the same age as their own children, they may notice that the language of their child is delayed. But if they do not have any means of comparison, it may be longer before they realize that something is wrong.

Deaf children should be taught to articulate a spoken language, but they cannot be expected to reach the same level. If a child has been able to hear even for a short period, perhaps less than a year, this greatly influences his possibilities of learning to articulate well. Such a child may reach a level of intelligible speech.

The greater the hearing loss, the more difficult it is for the child to learn to articulate well, but the child's various abilities for learning to articulate should also be considered. Children with apparently identical hearing losses may develop very different articulation skills.

Hearing aids may be of great help to children with some residual hearing. It may influence the rate of acquiring articulation skills as well as the intelligibility of their speach.

In order to articulate well one must be able to control the muscles of the chest (for controlling the airstream), the vocal cords, the muscles of the cheeks, the jaw, the tongue, and the lips. In natural acquisition of speech this control is mastered gradually, but a deaf child who has only used his voice for cries, often has no such control. It is a good idea before starting the actual speechtraining, to check the child's control of his lips and tongue. Exercises for training respiration are mentioned in connection with training lip movements, but apart from that, respiration comes in naturally with the very first vocalization exercises.

6

TEACHING HANDICAPPED CHILDREN

In this chapter we will describe practical methods of teaching handicapped children and youth. The methods are useful for most types and ages of handicapped students. Many of the methods are also suitable for non-handicapped students. The methods may be used in segregated or integrated classrooms. Group and individual methods of instruction are described.

CURRICULUM FOR HANDICAPPED STUDENTS

A suitable curriculum for handicapped students should have the following features.

1. *Ecological validity:* The curriculum must teach skills that are required in the environments in which students live now and in which they will likely live in future. Different skills are required of students living in village or city environments. Many of the skills required in one village may be different from those required in another village. In fact, many of the skills required of students living in one part of a city may be quite different from those required of students living in other parts of the same city. Many different skills are required in slum and

wealthy areas of a city. The curriculum must also teach the skills required of students in transition from one type of environment to another, for example, from village to city.

2. *Normalization:* Curricula must teach skills that will help students to lead lives that are as close as possible to the lives led by non-handicapped people. Students must be taught skills that will permit them to perform as independently as possible in the least restrictive environments in all areas of their lives. A least restrictive environment is one that is as close as possible to that in which non-handicapped people of the same chronological age generally perform. The curriculum must teach skills that will permit each student to integrate as much as possible with non-handicapped persons.
3. *Instructional validity:* The curriculum must teach functional skills. Functional skills are those that students require to live as independently, as age-appropriately and in a manner that is at least restricted as possible, now and in the future. The curriculum must also teach all of the skills that are prerequisite to learning each functional skill. An efficient curriculum should not include any skills that are not either functional or prerequisite to functional skills.

Ecological Inventory

An ecological inventory is a method of developing curricula that have all of the features listed above. The inventory is also used to develop criterion referenced tests. Tests and curricula developed by ecological inventories represent the ideal. In some situations, many of these methods may be readily adopted. In other situations the ideal may be difficult to achieve. In this case the ideal may represent a long-term goal to work toward.

The steps performed in an ecological inventory are as follows.

1. A target group of students is identified. A target group is a particular group of student for whom a curriculum or test is being developed. The target group is defined in terms of age, type of handicap, level of functioning and location (e.g., village or city). For example, separate ecological inventories would be required for: (*a*) children ages one month to three years; four-six years, etc.; (*b*) students with mild or severe mental retardation and (*c*) students living in villages, cities, poor or prosperous.
2. A survey is made of the home, community, school and vocational environments in which each student lives.
3. In each environment the subenvironments in which members of the target group are currently performing are identified. Also identified are the least restrictive environments in which the handicapped students could learn to perform in future. Least restrictive environments are as close as possible to those in which non-handicapped people of the same chronological age generally perform. For example, in a village community environment, subenvironments may include the fields where crops are grown, the village well, the market, the temple and the river where fish are caught.

   Usually, when predicting future environments, it will be sufficient to predict where students will be in one year, except where: (*a*) major environmental changes are predicted such as movements from rural to urban areas or (*b*) where a large number of skills are required and/or (*c*) where the skills required may take a long time to acquire, for example, vocational skills. In these cases, depending on the learning ability of the students in the target group, it may be desirable to predict where the students will be in three-five years.

4. The tasks in each subenvironment are then listed. For example, at the village well, tasks may include bathing (self or others), washing clothing, washing cooking equipment, and getting drinking and cooking water.

The analysis of subenvironments and tasks is performed through direct observation of behaviour in situations in which handicapped and non-handicapped students usually perform. In addition, parents and teachers may be interviewed to determine where, when and how students perform various tasks.

It may be wise to conduct the first inventory on the largest target group of handicapped students. The results of this first analysis will be useful to the largest number of students. Also, the largest group of students with handicaps will likely have the most similarities with other groups of handicapped students. As a result, the information from the first analysis will assist the analysis of other groups of handicapped students.

Before beginning a large analysis, it may be wise to conduct a limited study with a small number of students in a familiar environment such as the home. The analysis may be expanded to other environments and students following the development of efficient procedures.

To develop curricula that teach skills that are chronologically age-appropriate and that permit students to perform in the least restricted environments, ecological inventories are conducted of both handicapped and non-handicapped students of the same chronological age.

Functional tasks performed by non-handicapped students, that handicapped students could perform as a result of instruction or prosthetic (mechanical, electrical, sensory, motor or cognitive) assistance may be included in the curriculum.

This part of the analysis may be most efficiently conducted by following the steps listed below.

(a) Define the target group of students.

(b) Identify a broad variety of different types of families that have at least one handicapped child from the target group and at least one other non-handicapped child of the same sex and similar chronological age.

(c) Perform an ecological inventory on both the handicapped and non-handicapped children in each family; study both current and future environments and skills.

(d) Identify those functional tasks performed by the non-handicapped children that it is likely handicapped children could perform with prosthetic assistance or Instruction.

(e) Follow the steps listed below to decide if these tasks should be included in the curriculum being designed for students in the target group.

Curriculum Content

What skills should be in a curriculum for handicapped students? During an ecological inventory a survey is made of the tasks performed in home, community, school and vocational environments in which the students in the target group live. The tasks are listed according to their relative importance. These tasks are then task analysed to identify what specific skills to teach. These skills relate to a great variety of functional tasks in various environments. Some of the tasks that might be included in a curriculum designed for handicapped students living in a village are listed below. The list is not complete. The list does not apply to all villages. Note that some of the skills are used in only one environment. Other skills may be used in two, three or four environments.

Pre-school, early School and Severely Handicapped Students

Self-help, communication, gross and fine motor, cognitive (pre-academic or readiness), sensory, social and perceptual.

Older or higher functioning students

Arithmetic, reading (literature), language (writing, communication), history, geography, science, health and community living, arts and crafts, physical education, music, vocational.

Students with special handicaps

Speech reading, sign language and speech training for hearing impaired students.

Orientation, mobility and Braille for visually impaired students.

In the past these curricula have focused mainly on teaching academic or pre-academic skills. Often students have been given standard school curricula that they follow at a slower rate than do non-handicapped students. Recently, special curricula have been developed but they also tend to focus on academic and pre-academic tasks in addition to developmental tasks appropriate to students of younger chronological age levels.

Several problems arise with curricula of this type.

1. Some students never learn to read, write or do arithmetic well enough to use these skills in a functional way. Many hours are spent teaching

some students skills they cannot master and cannot use. This daily experience of failing to teach and failing to learn is very difficult for both teachers and students.

Because most of the students' time is taken trying to learn academic skills, little or no time is available to teach functional skills the students require in their everyday lives. As a result, the students are unsuccessful in all areas of life.

2. Some handicapped students do learn to perform some academic or pre-academic skills. Unfortunately, the classroom conditions in which the student learn these skills are different from the conditions in the natural environment in which the students must eventually perform the skills. Failure to generalize learning from the classroom to the natural environment is one of the major problems found when teaching handicapped students. Failure to generalize occurs when a student learns a skill in one situation but cannot perform the skill in another situation. For example, a student may learn to sort colour cards in the classroom but be unable to distinguish immature from ripe fruit on the basis of colour. The ability to distinguish red, green and blue on colour cards may not generalize to the selection of fruit because of:

   (a) the difference in format (no colour cards were used in the discrimination of the fruit);

   (b) slight differences between the colours of the cards and the colours of the fruit (the red fruit may have been a yellow-red); or

   (c) the failure to teach the learner the functional skill of choosing ripe fruit on the basis of colour.

Frequently, curricula that focus on teaching academics fail to give students enough practice under the variety of situations that occur in the natural environments. For example, to make colour discrimination a functional skill, one would not teach a student to sort colour cards (people are usually not required to sort colour cards in the natural environment). Instead the student would be taught to sort fruit and other objects that she or he will be required to sort on the basis of colour. Sorting colour cards is not a functional skill. Sorting fruit on the basis of colour is a functional skill. When a student is taught to sort colour cards the skill must transfer to a functional skill like sorting fruit. When a student is directly taught to sort fruit on the basis of colour, the student has been taught both how to sort colours and how to sort fruit on the basis of colour.

Problems with generalization to some extent affect all students. Problems with generalization increase as the level of intellectual functioning of the students decreases. Wherever possible, teach functional skills directly in the form in which they must be performed in the natural environment. Teaching skills in the natural environment is called in situ teaching. In situ teaching avoids many of the problems associated with generalization.

The intent is not to remove academics from the curriculum. Some handicapped students, particularly those who have visual, auditory or physical impairments may be able to achieve high academic levels including university. Some mentally retarded students may also be able to learn some very useful academic skills.

1. All handicapped students should be given the opportunity to learn the academic skills they are able to learn and that they will be able to use.
2. Ecological inventories should be done for all handicapped students to determine what academic skills they will need in the academic environments

they will likely move to in the future. For example, identify the knowledge and skills required in arithmetic, reading and science.

3. Each student's curriculum should teach the academic skills the student will require in the academic environments he will likely move to in future.
4. These academic skills should be learned and practised in the form in which they must eventually be performed. The problems of generalization may be reduced by teaching functional skills in the same form in which they must eventually be performed.
5. Organize the curriculum in terms of environments (e.g. home, community, vocational and school). Teach the functional skills required in each of these environments. A curriculum developed in this manner will result in each student being taught all of the academic skills they are capable of learning and using. In addition, each academic skill will be learned and practised in a functional form.
6. Teach each of the areas of the curriculum in proper proportion depending upon the nature of each student. For example, each year, review the skills required by each student in each of the environments. Determine what skills the student requires but does not have in his current environments, and what skills he will require but does not have in each of the future environments. Example programmes for three students are shown below. The amount of emphasis in each area of instruction is shown. All three students are ten years of age. Student one is blind and capable in the next year of passing to the next level of academic study. His long-term goal is to enter

university. His programme is mostly academic. He is also being taught a number of functional skills relating to the general community. A few skills functional in the home are also being taught.

Student two is moderately retarded. He has not learned many academic skills and will not likely learn many more. His long-term goal is sheltered employment and independence in the community and home. He will likely have considerable recreational time. There are many functional skills in the community and the home that he needs but does not have. His programme focuses on teaching functional and recreational skills for the community and home environments. As he gets a little older, the amount of emphasis in the vocational area may be increased.

Student three is physically handicapped and mildly mentally retarded. He is not strong in academic areas of performance and will likely not achieve a high academic level. He is capable of learning some additional practical academic skills to assist him in other areas of his life. With suitable training he will likely be able to gain independent employment. His programme is starting to focus on training vocational skills. He is also being taught a number of functional community skills.

The programmes for each of these students will be reviewed each year and the relative amount of emphasis in each area of instruction will be reviewed. The purpose of each programme is to train a student to be as functional as possible in each of the major areas of his or her life.

METHODS OF INSTRUCTION

Group Instruction

Individual instruction is often recommended as a method of teaching handicapped students. Individual instruction, however, has several disadvantages. First, it is relatively expensive. Second, it is often inefficient. Teacher attention is given to only one student at a time. Third, prolonged individual instruction on one task with one student often does not produce the best type of learning.

There is considerable evidence showing that group instruction can be used effectively with mildly, moderately, severely and even profoundly multiply, handicapped students. Furthermore, in many cases, there are several advantages to group instruction over individual instruction.

1. Group instruction is more efficient and less expensive., More students are often taught more effectively in the same period of time.
2. Various kinds of skills are often learned as rapidly.
3. In 'sequential' group instruction 'distributed practice' may improve 'maintenance' (recall of learning).
4. In sequential group instruction where students in the group are taught different skills, 'generalization' of learning may result. That is, students may learn the tasks being taught to other students in the group, observational learning.
5. When one student is rewarded for performing in a suitable manner, she or he acts as a good model for other students to imitate.

Two major types of group instruction are discussed below. The most suitable type of group instruction to use at a particular time depends upon the nature of the task and the students being taught. Different methods of group instruction may be suitable at various time. Usually, however, 'sequential' methods will be more suitable to students functioning at a low level of performance. While 'current' methods may be more suitable to higher functioning students. These students may have relatively well developed language skills and they may be more able to imitate a teacher's model or demonstration. Note, however, that even very severely, multiply handicapped students have been successfully taught with 'concurrent' methods. Sometimes students may begin with individual instruction, begin group instruction with the 'sequential' model and then move to the concurrent model of instruction.

Sequential Group Instruction

In sequential group instruction, several students (2 or more) are grouped close together. The students may be seated at desks in a semicircle, around a table, standing around the village well or in a field. Each student is taught independently for short periods. The teacher works briefly with one student then works briefly with another. During the total period of group instruction, the teacher will work several times with the same student.

Students in the group may be at the same or different levels of achievement. They may be taught the same or different skills. Each student may be treated entirely independently from the other students. Individualized methods of instruction may be used. Alternatively, the teacher may sometimes give general instructions or a demonstration at the same time to all students in the group before beginning sequential Instruction.

Sequential group instruction may provide a useful transition from individual to concurrent group instruction for students who are severely mentally retarded, multiply handicapped or who are simply inexperienced learners.

The benefits of this type of group instruction are as follows:

1. Each student receives individualization of instruction. The skills taught and the methods of teaching used are selected to suit each individual learner.
2. Each student receives several uninterrupted trials practising the same task (massed practice). Practice of this type (for a suitable period of time) helps to establish new skills.
3. After a brief period of either

   (a) inactivity,

   (b) observation of other students being instructed,

   (c) self-directed practice of a recently taught skill, or

   (d) a self-directed entertaining activity, the student is again introduced to the previously taught skill. Distributed practice of a skill makes a new skill more durable.
4. During sequential instruction, students may be taught a variety of skills required for concurrent group instruction. For example, the students may be taught to sit side-by-side for long periods without interfering with each other. They may be taught to focus more effectively on demonstrations, and listen to verbal instructions.
5. In sequential group instruction where students in the group are taught different skills, 'generalization' of learning may result. Students may learn the tasks being taught to the other students in the group, observational learning.

Concurrent group instruction

In concurrent group instruction, several students (two or more) are grouped close together. The students may be seated at desks in a semi-circle, around a table, standing around the village well or in a field. All students are taught by the teacher at the same time. This is the conventional form of group instruction. Concurrent group instruction may be introduced in stages using the previously described methods.

Students within the group must all be at the same general level of achievement. The students must all be able to learn from the same methods of teaching.

Individual Instruction

Individual methods of instruction may be used for teaching more difficult students in isolation from other students or during sequential group instruction. Also, some tasks requiring considerable individual assistance may be better taught through individual rather than group instruction. Attention, model, prompt and test teaching method may be used with modifications in individual instruction and in successive group instruction.

Prompts

A prompt is a type of temporary assistance used to help a student perform in a desired manner. When a student is unable to perform a task, a prompt (assistance) may be used to help the student perform. As the student learns to perform the task the temporary prompt is faded (slowly removed) from use. There are several different types of prompts: verbal, gestural, modelling and physical.

Task analysis

Task analysis is the process of analyzing a task into its parts. Task analysis is used to find out what steps should be taught so that a student will learn to perform a task. In an example, fish scaling was task analyzed. Five steps were found: (*a*) position the fish, (*b*) hold the fish by the tail, (*c*) position the knife, (*d*) scrape the fish, and (*e*) repeat until all the scales are gone. All of these steps must be performed in order to scale a fish. A chain is a set of steps that must be performed in order.

Rewards

Many people do long and hard tasks in the hot sun every day. They do things like plowing and digging, planting, carrying water, and picking and carrying crops. There is no one in the field giving them rewards because they did their job. They seem to do these tasks because it is their job.

Are these people rewarded for doing their work? Yes! Because they work, they get food or pay. With the food they and their family eat. Would they continue to work if they were not rewarded? No! If they did not get food or pay, they would not continue to work in the fields. People works because they get re-wards. Sometimes the reward is not immediate or direct.

Students work for rewards. Sometimes the reward is distant. The student believes that if he is successful in school he will get a better job. Some students are rewarded by their parents for getting good marks. Some students find school very difficult. They do not get good marks. They do not think they will get better jobs. They do not want to work in school because they do not get rewarded. Some handicapped students are like this.

When a handicapped student finds school difficult, when she or he fails, and is not rewarded, the student may quit trying to be successful. If a teacher wants this student to work harder doing a task the student does not want to do, the teacher will have to follow the steps listed below:

1. *Use shaping*. Ask the student to do what he can already do.
2.. *Use rewards*. Give the student a reward for trying to per-form the task.
3. Use shaping to help the student be successful.
4. Reward the student for being successful.
5. Later, when the student has been successful and when she or he has been taught that he will benefit from learning, the teacher may stop giving a reward. The student will continue to work because he will see the eventual rewards of his or her work.

What rewards can a teacher give to a student? A reward is something that a particular student will work to get. Some students will work very hard if a teacher smiles at them. The smile is a reward. The same smile may not reward another student. A student may do one task for a smile but may not do another task for a smile. If a teacher wants to reward a student for his work, the teacher must consider both the student and the task. The age of the student is an important consideration. What is rewarding in one culture may not be rewarding in another. Some things a teacher may give students are listed below. Teachers will have to test if these things are rewards—do they increase student effort:

1. *Verbal praise*. Describe what the student did well. Say things like, 'I am proud of you, you got four correct answers'. 'Good work, your printing is neat'. 'Good, your weaving is tight'. Use a variety of verbal praise, do not always say the same thing.
2. *Special privileges*. A student who performs well may be allowed to work at the teacher's table for a short time, sit for an hour in a special chair reserved for students who are working hard, or supervise or help younger students when they are working. The student may also be allowed to listen to a radio,

play with a special toy, read a special book or work on a craft. The student may be given a special hat to wear for the morning, be permitted to eat lunch with the teacher, or draw on the black-board. The student may be given extra paper or material for a craft project.

3. *Social praise.* When a student performs well the teacher may shake the student's hand, nod' and smile while giving verbal praise, or touch the student's shoulder. Often when a student performs poorly, a teacher will spend time talking to the student. The teacher's attention may increase the student's poor behaviour. Give teacher attention only to students who try hard or who show improvement. When a student performs well, a teacher may spend five minutes talking to the student about his interests.
4. *Food rewards.* When a student tries to perform well or improve even a small amount, the teacher may give the student part of a banana, some peanuts, some water or tea to drink. Many other things may be rewarding to different students, at different ages, in different cultures, at different times and tasks. Groups of teachers should discuss what might be rewarding for their students.

7

TEACHING CHILDREN WITH SPECIFIC LEARNING DISABILITIES

Specific learning disabilities have been recognized in some countries for much of the 20th century, in other countries only in the latter half of the century, and yet not at all in other places. Even where they have been recognized, the amount of help available varies from no services to their universal provision. This uneveness in intervention services is tragic since most persons with learning disabilities who receive sufficient, knowledgeable remediation can proceed through the school system and attain jobs that range from professor to labourer. Conversely, if they are not helped, the possibility of adjustment problems arising are considerable. As our world becomes more complex, the knowledge base increases and the concepts more abstract, an increasing number of people will experience difficulty and be assumed to have a learning disability. Our challenge will be to alter our parenting and teaching approaches so that their potential contribution to our collective lives is not forfeited.

Learning disabilities are formally defined in many ways in many countries. However, they usually contain three essential elements: a discrepancy clause, an exclusion clause, and anetiology clause. The discrepancy clause states there is a significant disparity between aspects of specific functioning and general ability; the exclusion clause states the disparity is not primarily due to intellectual, physical, emotional, or environmental problems; and the etiology clause speaks to causation involving genetic, biochemical, or neurological factors. This last clause is often stated in definitions, but it is not focused upon since it is difficult to determine etiology and usually is not part of the educational assessment or remedial programme recommended for the students.

The most frequent clause used in determining whether a student has a learning disability is the difference between areas of functioning. When a person shows a great disparity between those areas of functioning in which she or he does well and those in which considerable difficulty is experienced, this student is described as having a Learning Disability (LD). Persons of any intellectual level can have a learning disability, although most countries define a person with LD as having a near normal, or above normal intelligence. Persons with other handicaps also can have a learning disability, and thus are seen as multiply handicapped. LD can affect one or more of a person's areas of intelligence: language, spatial/ temporal visual, mathematics, knowledge of one's body and what it can do, social, or practical. Even when one's LAD appears to be confined primarily to a specific area of intelligence, frequently there are some problems in other areas of intellect. For example, the person who forgets the phone number she/he has read, also tends to forget the number s/he has been told.

When tasks in any area of intelligence are handled well, they are characterized by:

— advance planning,

— reflection, efficiency,

- economy (done with the least amount of backtracking),
- appropriate speed, adaptiveness, versatility, appropriateness for the context (particularly one's audience), insightfulness, social value, appropriate maturity, sophistication, complexity, judgement, focus, and elegance. When someone has a LD, one or more of these aspects break down.

AREAS OF DISABILITY

One of the ways that we can think about Learning Disabilities (LD) is to look at the ways the person with LD handles complexity, utilizes alternative approaches, attends to and remembers important information, uses appropriate judgement, thinks abstractly, notices the patterns in knowledge, and reflects upon what s/he is going to do, is doing, or has done. The following briefly explains what one is able to do when one functions well in each of the competencies:

1. *Complexity:* Copes with complex information or tasks, or several simultaneous tasks;
2. *Adaptivity and flexibility:* recognizes that there might be alternatives one has not considered, and uses them;
3. *Attends to and remembers the differences that make a difference:* notices which aspects of information are important and remembers them, ignores and forgets those of lesser importance; knows which agents accomplish what;
4. *Judgement:* effects judgements around which option to select, explanation to choose, behaviour to use;
5. *Symbolic thought:* ability to think about what language, punctuation, mathematical symbols, gestures, etc., represent, rather than think of them

concretely; ability to see generalities across spheres of knowledge; to perceive the patterns that connect knowledge;

6. *Perceives the patterns and rhythm of forms in knowledge:* is able to pace productions, distribute the content appropriately; is able to effect closure when part of the pattern is missing or has not been heard or noticed; and
7. *Reflection:* ability to think about one's actions in advance, in process and subsequently, and adjust one's productions accordingly; ability to make inferences from successes or failures.

Since LD are disabilities in specific areas of functioning rather than generalized intellectual deficits, we have to ask ourselves in which area or areas of functioning the person with LD has difficulty, and determine whether these problems occur in one or more competencies.

COGNITIVE FUNCTIONING

Handling Complexity

When persons with LD or Attention Deficit Disorder are faced with a number of tasks, or with a task they feel is complex, even if we, who can do it automatically, think it is easy, they may become overwhelmed and give up, or become overexcited, hyperactive, or misbehave. This also might occur if they are in an environment that is highly stimulating, noisy, novel, or confusing.

(a) Handling complexity linguistically

The language of a person with a language LD may become disorganized when they try to discuss a number of factors simultaneously. Alternatively, they may state a proviso, but lose the main point, or deviate onto a tangent and forget the main point. They might become confused when listening to a long or complex conversation, forgetting what has been said, or focusing on the inconsequential rather than the important points. They might have difficulty remembering all the parts of a multisyllabic word.

(b) Handling complexity

Spatially/Temporally persons with spatial/temporal LD may forget their way around a complex building, experience difficulty assembling a complex puzzle, or executing complex mechanical tasks, and remembering how others executed multifaceted tasks. Faced with such a task they may become overwhelmed and approach it randomly rather than plan fully. They may have difficulty finding objects when their surroundings are "busy", and may lack systems for storing, arranging, and finding their belongings.

They may have difficulty remembering the months of the year, which months have which number of days, the days of the week, or parts of the day.

(c) Handling complexity visually

Persons with visual LD may forget how words look, or how they are spelled, and so may forget how to read or spell words to which they have been previously exposed. Or they may recognize a word when they read it, but be unable to remember how to write it themselves. Forgetting how words look, the sounds in them, or how they are spelled may occur immediately after learning a word, after an hour or a day or two, or after an extended time. The LD student may have difficulty reading long words, forget the directions letters of idiograms face, or forget the shape of letters, numbers or ideograms. Just as the person with language LD may veer off topic when discussing a number of events, so may the person with visual LD lose the line from which s/he is reading print or music, and read content from another line.

(d) Handling complexity mathematically

Persons with math LD may forget number facts, and have difficulty holding math information in their heads while figuring out equations. They may become overwhelmed by a number of mathematical problems on a page.

(e) Handling knowledge of one's body

The person may be unable to replicate a complex task they have watched others perform, or remember a task they previously have performed. Some may be unable to do different tasks or movements with each hand simultaneously, or different movements of the hands and feet at the same time.

(f) Handling complexity socially

Some persons with LD may be overwhelmed by events involving a number of people or considerable stimulation, may have difficulty juggling several intimate and casual relationships appreciating the complexity of relationships, the fact that friends and intimates have good and bad features, disappoint us, and occasionally cannot be counted on. Instead they may concretely see people as being "good" or "bad" or forget information that is important to their friend.

(g) Handling complexity practically

In everyday aspects of functioning, persons with LD may have trouble imagining that they can juggle several tasks and chores simultaneously. They may lack a sense of how to juggle their social, vocational and practical commitments, forget what it is they have to do, may not know how to execute tasks efficiently, or how to block out several tasks so that the everyday aspects of their lives could be handled with the least amount of effort and on time.

Handling Tasks Adaptively/Flexibly

Persons with LD may think there is one fixed way to say or do something in their deficit area of functioning, so they do not necessarily realize or remember that there are alternatives. This contrasts with functional persons who see patterns and hence understand concepts; who recognize that language, mathematics, social interactions, everyday tasks, and the navigation or use of space can be approached in countless ways. Moreover, the poorly developed sense of pattern also means an inaccurate notion of outcomes, so that the LD rigidly cling to the narrow approaches with which they are familiar, and outcomes they can predict accurately.

(a) Language

Persons with language LD may not select another way of expressing themselves if what they said was misunderstood or poorly received. Their vocabulary may be more limited than that of other members of their family so they may not have a repertoire of alternative words and phrases they could use, or may forget the words they have heard or do know. They may not understand what has been said if the provision precedes the condition, such as, "Before you come in the door, take your shoes off." Others may use the same phrases over and over, or talk about the same topic endlessly.

(b) Spatial/Temporal

Persons with spatial/temporal LD may be unable to find their way around a building if they enter from a different door. It might not occur to them there are alternative possibilities for organizing their spoken or written language, their belongings and files, for organizing their tasks or chores more efficiently, or initiating tasks earlier so they are completed on time. They may not realize there is a more functional way to approach a mechanical task, may not distribute their clothing attractively on their bodies, set out an attractive party table, or have noticed or remembered how others do this.

(c) Visual

Persons with visual LD may not distribute their written or art work appropriately on the page so it may be too large or small run off the page, or may not distribute their work effectively in their notebook. They may not be aware of alternative ways of decoding a word they do not recognize. They may fail to use the index to find information in a book. Instead, they may search randomly.

(d) Mathematics

Persons with LD may do mathematics in a rote fashion rather than recognize the many possible approaches leading to the same outcome. They may always use the same strategy regardless of how efficient or effective it may be, or have difficulty understanding questions that are arranged horizontally rather than vertically.

(e) Knowledge of body

Some may have one way of executing a task, however inefficient: may be unaware of different ways of using their bodies to do things, as a form of expression or gesture, or may not have noticed or remembered how others do so.

(f) Social

Other persons with LD may have a limited repertoire of social behaviours which bore people, rather than adjusting behaviour to context and adapting it if it is not received as expected. They may distribute content of social language inadvisably, telling an acquaintance everything about themselves when they first meet, or pace intimacy inappropriately such as proposing marriage on the second date. Some may lack an accurate sense of extended time and of a lifespan, and may not have noticed how others pace content and intimacy, which contributes to difficulties with pacing. Others may lack alternative possibilities for solving interactional problems, may see each of their values as being equally important, and so be unwilling to negotiate or compromize. Some may not recognize that outcomes are worked on together. Some LD's may be perseverative—which is to repeat a topic too frequently or to talk at too great length about a topic rather than discuss their audience's interests, or vary their repertoire. Others may fail to change their image of themselves, of others and of relationships as they, others and contexts change; may not understand how family relationships work, e.g., how they are related to their grandparent or uncle; may have difficulty understanding situations from other's points of view.

(g) Practical

Persons with LD may be unaware that there are alternative ways of organizing one's practical tasks including short cuts. When time is limited, they may rigidly resist reallocation of priorities to ensure the most important tasks will be completed. Others may not know which friends and intimates would be prepared to do some of their tasks occasionally.

Remembering the Differences that make a Difference/ Judgement

Whenever someone has a LD in an area of functioning,

they tend not to notice and/or remember important detail in that area. They may notice and remember inconsequential information which clutters their memory span with items that others would forget. Others may lack judgement concerning what is important or where importance tends to occur, so they study everything, or fail to prioritize and reprioritize. This results in disorganization, inefficiency, failure to complete tasks and feeling overwhelmed.

Since everyone with LD fails to notice some detail in their deficit area, virtually everyone with LD has an attentional problem. On the other hand, people with attentional problems do not necessarily have LED Attentional problems and/or hyperactivity also can be manifestations of an Attention Deficit Disorder, Developmental Disability, Sociopathy, immaturity, depression, or anxiety.

(a) Language

Persons with LD may not know when in the lesson or semester important information will be conveyed, so effect poor judgments about when to be attentive. They may not notice the differences between similar sounding phonemes such as "ch"/"sh", "k"/"g", v"/"f", which is reflected in their speech and spelling. May forget some of the syllables in words so leave them out when speaking or writing, may not notice the meaning of pauses or silence so control conversation by a continuous barrage of speech. Others may forget the order of syllables, saying "hangover" instead of "overhang", or use an incorrect word such as ""reincarnate" instead of "remembrance". They may not notice voice inflection that indicates meaning, and therefore do not necessarily pick up on humour or sarcasm. Some persons with LD forget meaningful language—in which case their problems may be conceptual rather than memory—whereas others forget rote language such as a telephone number. Some may mention every detail when talking instead of selecting the points that their audience needs to know or would be interested in, and write about every facet. Others may lose the central point because they become distracted by tangents or by background noise or speech.

(b) Spatial/Temporal

LD persons may not notice landmarks in space which would help them find their way in a community or building, may not notice the distinctive aspects of people's faces or bodies so they could be recognized subsequently, may not notice the clothing and accessories that others in their group are wearing, nor how they are arranged on their bodies. Some may not notice how others cut their hair, use gesture, movement or social space. Others may not have noticed how others block their time out, or what is involved in doing a task, so they may overestimate the amount of time needed to complete tasks, becoming overwhelmed at what they have to do, or underestimate the amount of time, leaving tasks to the last minute and becoming stressed and discouraged. Some may not have noticed how others preplan the use of space on a page or preplan errands to ensure there is no backtracking, or may not have noticed the patterns of a day or week, what typically occurs at 9 a.m. or on a Saturday.

(c) Visual

Some may not have noticed the direction specific letters face the direction in which to read or write, the sequence of letters in a word, how a word looks or is spelled, how punctuation is used the size of sentences in different contexts, how paragraphs are used, the use of underlining, or where important content is likely to be found in a textbook, novel, play, etc. When checking their work, they may not notice their errors or omissions.

(d) Mathematics

Others may not notice the difference between a multiplication or addition sign, or how the various types of equations are spaced such as the indentation of numbers in multiplication, nor comprehend why such discriminations are important.

(e) Knowledge of body

LD persons may not notice that their hair is messy, their face dirty, buttons improperly aligned, shirt untucked, etc. They may not notice pain or be aware that they have a rash, cut or infection, or notice when they are hungry or satiated, may not attend to detail when bathing or cleaning their teeth. Others may be restless, impatient, have a short attention span, be hyperactive or hypoactive (underactive, lethargic, very disorganized).

(f) Social

Some LD students may not notice subtle social behaviours such as impatience or hints, or the subtleties of relationships such as what people do to maintain friends or express caring, or what friends and intimates contribute to relationships such as support. Others may be impervious to others' reactions to their behaviour, and insensitive to others' needs.

(g) Practical

Some may not notice house cleaning that needs doing or groceries that need buying, or may not have noticed the systems that others utilize for arranging the practical aspects of their lives.

Thinking Symbolically

Persons with LD always experience difficulty thinking symbolically in their deficit area of functioning. They fail to notice the patterns that connect knowledge, be those patterns the many equations whose answer is "8", that division is the opposite of multiplication, or that words consist of parts, each of which conveys meaning. They do not notice the pattern of a chapter in a textbook or a mystery so they are unaware of which types of information can be found at which juncture, and therefore, which parts to skim and which to read carefully because they are important. They may not notice the typical pattern of a teacher's class, so are uncertain of what will occur when; they do not know when their attention can and must not wander. Since they have this hazy sense of pattern, they do not build the anticipation that encourages people who are not LD to persist with the task until the end.

Because their world is unpredictable, they cling to whatever is familiar, either dreading outcomes or being too casual about them, and so fail to prepare for them. Their hazy sense of pattern and hence of pace, distribution and rhythm results in errors of quantity so they provide too little or too much information, write too little or too much, or are too active or insufficiently active.

(a) Language

The LD person may interpret language literally so they misunderstand what someone is saying. They think of and write about the most concrete aspects of concepts rather than about the abstract ideas that the concepts represent, or they may connect unrelated information, or misunderstand the meaning of some words, and so make erroneous assumptions. Some may not understand the concepts behind words so that an adult with LD thought that scientists who were not natural scientists were unnatural scientists.

Others may not have noticed typical form in their own language. A 13-year-old English speaking girl, when asked how many ears she had, responded with "13". A 13-year-old who did not have a LD would recognize that if someone wanted to know her age, they would ask, "How old are you?" not "How many years do you have?", since the latter is not the form (pattern) that English speakers use. Since the LD may not have noticed the patterns that others use when they speak, they may not describe events in an organized, sequential, and understandable manner. Other persons with LD may not realize that how they say something carries more meaning than what they say.

Because of their difficulties with pattern, some may not be able to break language into its parts such as the child who thought that "hurtyourknee" was one word. Others are unable to tease out the sounds that make up a word. Systems are patterns as well, so that the LD are unsystematic in their approaches, e.g., rather than memorize information cumulatively with each additional piece of information to memorize, they may start at the beginning.

Spoken language is an abstract representation of experience. Written language is a further abstraction of spoken language. Some persons with LD experience difficulty with reading and writing because they lack the concept that written language is a condensation and selection of experience geared to a specific audience. Some persons have such severe language LD that they lack the language to think about abstract notions such as "truth", "loyalty", or "love". This interferes with their conceptual development which, in turn, limits the maturation of their language. Many persons with LD are unaware that the essential reason for speaking and writing is to communicate with others. This includes negotiating outcomes with others, making ourselves increasingly understood, sharing experience, maintaining our relationships, and providing and seeking stimulation and information.

(b) Spatial/Temporal

Students with LD may be unaware of how and why buildings and communities are laid out in a predictable fashion, and so are unable to find their way around a familiar building community, or one that is similar to those they have encountered. They have no sense of why people organize belongings systematically—be they toys, notes, clothing, or files and so are unable to find things in others' homes, or modify others' systems for their own use. Some may be unaware that people pre-organize language given who they are conversing with, and the context in which they are interacting. Others may have difficulty understanding language that uses spatial relationships such as "beside", "taller than Lilly but shorter than Jay," or following instructions that involve movement or manipulating materials in space. LD students may have difficulty understanding or using terms that occur in time, such as "consequently" or "yesterday", or understanding cause-effect language. They may not comprehend abstract representations of space such as geography and geometry; how the information on a map is translated into geographic space; may not know which state or continent they live in; may forget which side of the road traffic comes from; may not understand terms like north, south, east, west; may not understand what we convey to others in our use of social space and so may stand too close or too far, or touch too frequently or infrequently. They may classify objects of events in terms of superficial or tangential characteristics.

Students with learning disabilities may be unaware of how and why people organize, prioritize and reprioritize their time. Some have a poor sense of what time is about, that clock, calendars, and date books indicate the passage of time, and that days weeks, months, and years punctuate time. They may be unaware that units of time such as a minute, hour, or century are fixed, or be unaware of what a century or millenium stand for, or what "19" means in "1993".

(c) Visual

Some students with LD may not understand how written language is constructed, what some words and parts of words mean, the many ways that meaning can be determined, or which parts of words, sentences, or paragraphs can and cannot have their sequence altered. They also may not realize how meaning is determined when reading, therefore making wild guesses about the meaning of words; may lack a system for copying from the blackboard, or may have difficulty relating science diagrams to experiments or to written data.

(d) Mathematics

LD students may not understand that mathematics is a language of quantity, or comprehend what various operations such as subtraction do and why, or what concepts such as equivalency mean. They may not know the meaning of zero, comprehend what fractions are, understand the amounts that the denominations of money stand for, or be able to measure cooking ingredients. Some may not notice the positions in space that are used to convey meaning in the decimal system, or may be confused by the wording of mathematics problems, and so do not extract the important data.

(e) Knowledge of body

Other LD students may be unaware of the messages conveyed by eye contact, facial expression, movement, use of social space, gesture, dress and grooming, or how others react to those aspects of themselves. They may misinterpret others' expressions and gestures, and therefore, their intent, may have poor sense of the size and shape of their bodies, and what their bodies can do. Others may forget the names of body parts.

(f) Social

Students with learning disabilities may have difficulty appreciating what different relationships give and mean to people, and what different friends and relatives expect. They may not understand the symbolic (or metaphorical) aspects of maturing relationships such as substituting "keeping in touch" for direct touching. Others may not have noticed that people negotiate outcomes together, and so may be controlling rather than collaborative. Some may not understand how family relationships work such as what a grandparent or in-law is, that people continue to be brothers or sisters when they are adults, or after they are dead.

(g) Practical

Some may have no notion of why people organize their use of time or their tasks, or that they take the expectations of the important persons in their lives into account when deciding how organized to be, how attentive to be and in which contexts, and what events and items to remember.

Using Reflection/Imagery

Persons with LD may not realize that others use inner language to preplan what they are going to say or do, to critique their language and actions as they are saying and doing them, and to reflect upon what they have done after it is completed, so that their productions always are in the process of being refined. Nor do they look at the total picture before undertaking a task; they may fail to analyse conditions or identify salient relationships upon which to base a hypothesis.

(a) Language

Some persons with LD may not realize that others pre-organize their language before speaking, choosing what they will say and how they will say it based upon their own priorities and the priorities they think their audience has, the impression they want to make, the age and sophistication of their audience, what their audience probably knows so does not have to be told, and what they think their audience thinks of them. Nor may they realize that people watch others' reactions to their language and actions, and change what they are doing or saying in process. As a result, their language may be confusing to their listener because it provides too little or too much information, is too sophisticated or complex, or is unduly simple. Without meaning to, they may be tactless, offensive, boring, or fail to address what the audience was seeking others may react to situations impulsively without thinking about what response would be most favourably received.

(b) Spatial/Temporal

Students with LD may not be aware that others tasks and use of time, use preventative planning such as taking items to school before they are needed or making lists, or that others have contingency plans. Their productions, be they verbal, written, vocational or instrumental, may not reflect the priorities of others with whom they live or work. They may not problem solve the way they do their tasks or their use of time, so that tasks are combined and sequenced to conserve time and energy, and the most important given priority. One adult with LD each day purchased the ingredients for the lunch he took to work, rather than buying a supply for several days. They may have difficulty reconstructing their actions in order to remember where they put something, may jump into tasks or games without listening to the instructions, or before the instructions are completed. Others may fail to preplan the ways they could use space, be it on a page, in a book, or organizing items in their home.

(c) Visual

Some LD persons may fail to check their work, or modify their productions in light of what they have learned from previous successes or failures. Assignments might be a poor reflection of teachers' or bosses' expectations in terms of length, neatness, organization, content, or style.

(d) Knowledge of body

Persons with LD may not preplan what they will wear, critique the appropriateness of their attire or their state of cleanliness and neatness, or may not take into advance consideration the impact their gestures, movement, and use of social space will have on others.

(e) Mathematics

Some may attack a mathematics problem without a careful assessment of what the language of the problem is requesting, or may copy numbers and math signs incorrectly, and not notice their errors.

(f) Social

Failing to take their audience into account before producing a social behaviour is a problem for some LD persons. They may not reflect on the impact of their behaviour on others, and modify appropriately. As a result, their behaviour may be egocentric, impervious, and inappropriate.

(g) Practical

LD students may not reflect on whether important tasks and chores are being completed efficiently, on time, and sufficiently well to be acceptable to friends, intimates, fellow workers, and job supervisor.

SPECIFIC TEACHING STRATEGIES FOR LD STUDENTS

Given the general principles and suggestions on global strategies described above, we will now look at more specific remedial suggestions in each of the seven areas of intellectual competencies.

Language

Language is the most essential of the intellectual competencies. It is usually composed of four individual abilities: listening speaking, reading, and writing with development occurring in this order.

(a) Listening

Listening involves attending, processing information, and having enough knowledge of vocabulary and content to put a speaker's speech into a meaningful form. Learning disabled students often do not attend effectively and so even if they have the other skills, they do not understand the discourse. Problems with attention and distractibility are found in many LD students. There are many ways that help alleviate this that include:

(i) Reduce verbal distractions. Have the student sit in a quiet part of the classroom, practice listening to only one other student, then to a small group;

(ii) Have the student maintain constant eye contact with the teacher or peers that are talking. If your culture does not encourage eye contact, sit beside the student and speak quietly so he/she has to

attend if he/she is to understand what you are saying;

(iii) Have the student sit close to the front of the class—this naturally blocks out much distraction;

(iv) Schedule difficult lessons when the student is most alert;

(v) Allow the student to move around if this helps him/her concentrate; and

(vi) Give short assignments and try to provide immediate feedback.

Listening also involves being able to process discourse. This includes hearing words clearly, perceiving them accurately, and remembering the passage in order. LD students do not have hearing difficulties as a primary disorder, but some do have problems with auditory discrimination. For example, a student may confuse the words 'patience' and 'impatience'. You can help a student by facing him/her, saying the words distinctly, and speaking slowly so he/she can process all the parts of the word. Perceiving the words clearly can be difficult. Transposing sounds is a well-known problem for the LD student. You may be talking about 'form' but he/she will hear 'from'. These students are helped by repeating words or by listening to words on a tape recorder. Another approach is to say one word, follow it by a pair containing the original one, and then asking the student to identify the correct one.

The last important skill in processing discourse is being able to remember a sequence pattern. For example, the teacher may say, "Good morning children, take off your coat, come to the circle, and we will talk about our day." The student may remember each part of the instruction but not in correct sequence, so he/she may come to the circle, and then take off his/her coat.

Or he/she may only remember the first and last phrase and not know where to go. This student can be helped by embedding the instruction in a classroom routine. If this opening activity is always the same and you express it in the same verbal manner each morning, the LD student can learn the sequence. Once this is accomplished, you can add additional parts or change the instruction, one part at a time.

The third aspect of listening involves knowing the vocabulary and context in which it is being used. Experiential approaches to language are helpful because the student can use words and experiences she or he is familiar with. If she has just had a birthday party, she will listen more carefully to a story about a classmate's party or about a party in the story the teacher is reading.

Listening is often a problem for the LD student because the discourse is too complex, the words too difficult, the sentences too long, and the concepts not fully understood. The student may understand the parts, but is unable to construct the whole. For example, if the teacher is talking about 'black holes', the LD student will understand the individual words but not know that the teacher is talking about dungeons.

(b) Speaking

Speaking is the second aspect of language with which the LD student has difficulty. By the time a student is in grade one, most students can speak approximately 3,000 words and understand 15,000. Effective parents have expanded their children's language by using their vocabulary and context, and modelling an extension. For example, the child may say 'Me want milk" to which the mother replies, "Yes dear, you want some milk". There is never a negative response from the mother, but a model of a better way of saying the same thing. This approach to expand language by the teacher is also appropriate especially when the goal is to help the LD student use correct grammar.

Summarizing events or passages read by the teacher or peers is an excellent way to improve both speaking and reading comprehension. This will be expanded in the reading section, but suffice to say that summarizing is rarely expected in the regular classroom. But when it is, the LD student gains in all aspects of language.

(c) Reading

There are three essential aspects of reading: decoding, comprehension, and speed. The LD student may have difficulty with each. Decoding is the first and most crucial skill. If the student does not have this skill, he/she needs to use most of his/her working memory figuring out letters, syllables, words, and sentences. Basal programs that are well structured are usually most appropriate for the LD students. The first step is to match sounds to letters and to rehearse unfit it is automatic. After this, combining consonants and vowels in ever increasing quantity allows the teacher to build up the students repertoire. For example, start with 1. CV and VC combinations (ta, at), 2. CVC VCC, VCV, VVC (cat, off, ate, eat); 3. CVCV, CCVT, CVCC (late, clot, kiss) and so on. In some languages, there are also syllables and words that do not follow the sound/letter sequence and require practice with sight methods. For example, sight where the fight' makes the 'it' sound, or thorough where sough' makes the 'ow' sound. Many schools have books that have ordered letters, syllables, and words for you to use in working with LD students.

In addition to learning how to decode sounds and words, the student also has to learn the meaning of the vocabulary and comprehend the entire sentence, paragraph, and passage. Research has shown that students are able to learn and remember material they are familiar with more efficiently than material with which they are unfamiliar. For example, most countries have a sport that is popular across the nation. Learning words that identify with that sport and reading stories about it make reading more interesting. In India, hockey is our national sport. Words like 'puck', 'stick', 'goalie', 'team', 'ice' are usually easy to learn because they are already in the lexicon of most students.

In addition to teaching LD students the sounds that make up words and the vocabulary that leads to comprehension, it is also important to make the student personally responsible for his or her own approach to reading. Reciprocal reading is an approach that focuses on making students move from being dependent to independent in their reading activity. Palinczar has developed a programme that includes four aspects:

(i) summarizing—where the student is asked to summarize the passage being read;

(ii) questioning—involves asking who, what, when, where, how, and why, such as 'what are we reading?'

(iii) predicting—asks what is coming next or what is the title of this story and so on; and

(iv) clarifying—which asks the student to define difficult words or shows how to use context clues.

(d) Writing

The last aspect of language is writing. Many LD students become skillful in speaking, listening, and reading, but continue to have problems with writing, especially as they get older and the writing demands increase. A basic approach to improving writing is to have students write more. Scardamalia and Bereiter have observed that LD students spend considerable time writing before the quality of their work improves. Students with learning disabilities usually need practice in both the technical and narrative aspects of writing. Fluency in writing is also required. Timed exercises as described in reading are also useful. Having students write anything for two minutes increases their quantity. You may want to structure this as you did with reading, starting with single letters, words, and sentences. This introduces an automaticity into writing that is necessary before LD students become fluent writers. It also introduces students to observing and practising the patterns in writing.

The technical aspects of writing include punctuation, handwriting, grammar or style of writing, and spelling. LD students need to understand that the rules of punctuation are important not just in making their writing look well, but also to mark the language groupings that aid comprehension to reduce the complexity of the task. The most basic rules of punctuation are that sentences start with capital letters and end with periods. Within sentences, commas break up the parts that help the student read and write in rhythm. Understanding this helps the student organize his or her work and that of others. Once the students can use the basic punctuation rules effectively, they can go on to use more complex forms such as semicolons, colons, quotation marks, question marks, exclamation marks and so on.

Handwriting is important for both the reader and writer. Many LD students have problems with fine motor coordination skills that interfere with adequate writing. Approaches that can be helpful are:

(i) to practise with large lined sheets of paper, copying words that the teachers have modelled, many times over

(ii) use manuscript rather than cursive form when writing. Letter by letter is often clearer and just as

fast once the student has practised often enough to become fluent. If the student feels this is a form that only young children use, teach him/ her to join letters—a form of print that works well and is easier than learning the cursive form, e.g., turn becomes school becomes

Many LD students need considerable practice in both spelling and decoding individual words. This is often referred to as over teaching and over learning. The words that require this approach are those that are most frequently used in both reading and writing.

Grammar may be a serious problem for the LD students. Agreement of verb tense throughout a written passage and agreement between subject and predicate are the most basic errors made by LD students. Most teachers do not penalize students for these, but they should correct them. While these errors are found so frequently, many LD students do not have a correct imprint to refer to when they are writing. This is especially true when they are in whole language programs that use students' writing as their reading base rather than commercial materials. Students should practice correct grammar forms through continual repetition and thorough knowledge of the rules that govern correct grammar.

A frequently used cognitive strategy for LD students who need techniques for technical editing is COPS. This approach has been developed in the learning disability institute at the University of Kansas. COPS is a mnemonic that helps LD students remember the essential aspects of editing.

- *C* represents Capitalization
- *O* represents the Organization and Orderliness of the story;
- *P* represents Punctuation- and

— *S* represents Spelling.

When a student finishes the first draft of a written passage, he/ she should then 'do a COPS' for technical correcting. The teacher may have to remind the student to do this initially, but eventually it should become internalized.

Young LD children often show good oral language; in fact, the discrepancy between their written and spoken language may be one of the ways of identifying students as learning disabled. As these same students grow older, however, they have fewer experiences with written and oral language. Adults do not read to them, and their own ability to read and write is at a much lower level than their developmental age would predict. Non-handicapped students are not always taught how to write well, but most pick up skills spontaneously; students with learning disabilities need to be taught directly. For example, if an older student is expected to answer questions on a test in history, he or she should know how to summarize important topics in the course and retrieve them at examination time. If the student is expected to answer a question that asks for an opinion or argument, the student should be directly taught a structure. For example, the teacher would teach the following format:

(i) opening statement of student's opinion on the question;

(ii) three statements that support the opinion;

(iii) statement of contrary opinion;

(iv) reconciliation of contrary opinion and student's own;

(v) concluding statement that reaffirms the initial statement.

Many learning disabled students have poor

organizational skills and poor sense of time. If the teacher expects them to do a project in science, the specific content may not be the problem. What is involved in the project, how it is to be organized, and what time frame is required are often more problematic. A student who has difficulty with attention and perseverance may be in trouble before he/she even starts. Judging what is possible and planning a personal timetable will be essential. The teacher often needs to help the LD student plan these features. For example, if the grade five project demands five hundred words with illustrations and must be submitted to the teacher at the end of the month, the LD students will need organizational support in several areas. The first is time. The teacher has assigned a project at the beginning of the month so the student has four weeks to complete it (lots of time, he or she thinks). If this is to be a successful experience, however, the teacher has to help the student find a topic, design a cover page, show where to look for reference materials, decide on illustrations, decide what to include, develop a timetable for meetings with the teacher, and a personal timetable so that everything will be done within the month. All students would benefit from this, but for the LD student, it is essential.

Narrative writing is part of the language programme for many students from grade one through secondary school. We discussed some of the technical support skills earlier; now we will address the composition itself. In many countries, students are asked to use their own experiences from which to develop stories. For those whose creative skills need to be augmented brainstorming ideas and vocabulary can be especially helpful for the learning disabled student.

8

SPECIAL EDUCATIONAL NEEDS OF GIFTED/TALENTED CHILDREN

Before beginning to develop provision for gifted and talented students it is necessary to understand just what is meant by these terms, and how they apply to children in our classrooms. There is large variation in the range and breadth of definitions of gifted and talented students, and little consensus on a satisfactory definition. The concept of giftedness is at times difficult to defend because it is defined too loosely while being measured too restrictively.

DEFINITIONS OF GIFTEDNESS AND TALENT

Originally the words gifted and talented were often used interchangeably, or at times the concept of "talent" was seen as being in some way lesser compared with the idea of giftedness. For example, M.J. Morelock referred to a hierarchical categorization with "talent" referring to specialized aptitudes that are assumed to be unrelated—and inferior—to general intelligence and giftedness. In the mid 1990's, the term "talented" was often used to replace "gifted", which was thought to have connotations of "getting something for nothing", or being specially chosen in some way. J Freeman and Winstanley comment that the term "gifted" often seems to have religious overtones of gifts bestowed by God. Winstanley also remarks that this also implies moral connotations to do with being gifted, as if the child has a responsibility to apply themselves and not waste their abilities. The term "able" and variations of it are used frequently in the educational literature as it is felt to be more appropriate and less emotive. In both Wales and Scotland pupils are classified as "More Able and Talented" and "Able" respectively. Winstanley notes that the term "able" is often prefixed by words such as "more", "very", "severely" or "profoundly", in order to create subtle distinctions that are often neither objective nor useful. She advocates using the term "highly able" for the majority of able pupils and "exceptionally able" for those who are particularly outstanding.

However, the terms "gifted" and "talented" are those that are used most frequently in government strategies and research literature and so will be used in the rest of this review. F. Gagné differentiated between the concepts of gifted and talented by defining giftedness as above-average competence in human ability, and talent as above-average performance in a particular field. Giftedness refers to human aptitudes such as intellectual or creative abilities. Talent however is demonstrated in an area of human activity such as mathematics, literature or music. Freeman echoes this definition, adding that gifts are usually easy to measure as intellectual aspects of development, whereas talents are normally discovered by experts in those fields. This can be further clarified by Munro's distinction between talented students as displaying exceptional ability in areas in which they have been explicitly taught, and gifted students as those who display exceptional ability in certain areas without explicit teaching. Thus it follows that a gifted student may not necessarily be defined as talented. In 1988, the US Congress defined gifted and talented as:

> "The term "gifted and talented students" means children and youth who give evidence of high performance capability in areas such as *intellectual, creative, artistic,* or *leadership* capacity, or in specific academic fields, and who require services or activities not ordinarily provided by the school in order to fully develop such capabilities"

Deborah Eyre provides a simpler definition: "An able child, as defined by our school, is one who achieves, or has the ability to achieve, at a level significantly in advance of the peer group. This may be in all areas of the curriculum or in a limited range."

As of 2005 the current definitions from the Department for Education and Skills in Great Britain (DfES) are as follows:

Gifted: The top 5-10 per cent of pupils per school as measured by actual or potential achievement in English, Maths, Science, History, Geography, Modern Foreign Languages, RE, ICT or Design and Technology.

Talented: The top 5-10 per cent of pupils per school as measured by actual or potential achievement in the subjects of Art, Music or PE.

However one element of this description should be emphasized: it is the top 5-10 per cent of pupils *per school, regardless of the overall ability profile of pupils.*

Categories of Definitions of Giftedness

D. McAlpine classified definitions of giftedness according to three criteria; whether they are conservative or liberal; single- or multidimensional; and whether they are based on potential or performance.

Conservative versus liberal

Conservative definitions tend to restrict the areas that are included in the categorization of giftedness or talent, or how many people will be regarded as gifted—for example the top 5 per cent of any given measure of ability. These definitions also tend to use a single dimension such as high intelligence, to define giftedness. More liberal definitions would suggest that there is no meaningful difference between those who score in the top 3-5 per cent, and the 10-15 per cent who come just below and so would advocate that 15-20 per cent should be included in the gifted category.

Single- versus multidimensional

Some definitions of giftedness refer to ability in just one domain, usually academic, while others include achievements in a number of domains. The more domains that are included the more liberal the definition could be considered to be. While a broad definition of giftedness is desirable as it makes it less likely that individuals who are gifted will be overlooked, it is also necessary to guard against creating a definition so broad that everyone is regarded as gifted, undermining the exceptionality of the individual.

Potential versus performance

Some definitions require concrete evidence of above average performance. Others include children, for example those who are underachieving, whose performance may not be exceptional but who would be considered to have further potential. Freeman remarked that the inclusion of the word "potential" in within a definition of gifts and talents, rather than only recognized performance, often serves to diminish the "elitist" nature of many definitions.

Culture and context

Along with these categories it should be remembered that the ideas of giftedness and talent and dependent on both culture and context. Which categories of definition are advocated internationally depends on the educational culture and school system of that particular country. On a more local scale, and because the term gifted is always a comparison, children can be called gifted at very different levels of achievement. In highly selective schools some children might be viewed as "stupid" by classmates, whereas they might be termed "gifted" in other schools.

IDENTIFYING GIFTED AND TALENTED STUDENTS

Clear, objective and useful criteria are needed in order to identify the most able pupils in education and provide for their needs. However, the vast array of definitions, as well as common prejudices about what constitutes giftedness/talent can often hamper the establishment of these guidelines. Giftedness is often equated with high IQ, and yet IQ measures alone may not pick up the all of the highly able children in a classroom setting. A number of researchers have proposed checklists of characteristics, implying that it should be possible to simply tick boxes pertaining to the attitudes and behaviours of pupils. Winstanley notes however, the desire to be inclusive means that the checklists are often unwieldy, too vague to be useful and at times completely contradictory. To give an example of this below are elements from two checklists displayed side-by-side:

Able pupils are likely to

Demonstrate unusual curiosity	*Exhibit boredom*
Finish work with ease and speed	Take extra time to finish tasks to a high standard
Have many friends	Be quite isolated
Contribute willingly in class	Refuse to comply with instructions
Be interested in a broad variety of topics	Only express interest in a narrow range of subjects

These examples are taken from Eyre and the DfES website "Excellence in Cities", and are reported in Winstanley. They are a good illustration of why gifted children cannot be treated as a homogeneous group and caution those who seek to describe them according to a set of pre-defined attributes. Checklists can be valuable instruments for stimulating thought and they may spark recognition in teachers for pupils perhaps not previously considered gifted.

GENERAL CHARACTERISTICS OF GIFTED, TALENTED AND MORE ABLE PUPILS

Many educationalists have produced lists of characteristics of very able children. Familiarity with these characteristics can help teachers to build up a pupil profile of learning strengths. Such a profile may help to identify a pupil who might not be achieving at a particularly high level but who may have real ability in certain areas. He or she may:

- be a good reader
- be very articulate or verbally fluent for their age
- give quick verbal responses
- have a wide general knowledge
- learn quickly
- be interested in topics which one might associate with an older child
- communicate well with adults—often better than with their peer group
- have a range of interests, some of which are almost obsessions
- show unusual and original responses to problem-solving activities
- prefer verbal to written activities

- be logical
- be self taught in their own interest areas
- have an ability to work things out in their head very quickly
- have a good memory that they can access easily
- be artistic
- be musical
- excel at sport
- have strong views and opinions
- have a lively and original imagination / sense of humour
- be very sensitive and aware
- focus on their own interests rather than on what is being taught
- be socially adept
- appear arrogant or socially inept
- be easily bored by what they perceive as routine tasks
- show a strong sense of leadership
- are not necessarily well-behaved or well liked by others

None of these behaviours are proof of high ability but they may alert teachers to the need to enquire further into a pupil's learning patterns and ability levels.

Parent's Reports

Parents often have a detailed knowledge of their children's abilities, and can be a very useful source of information in identifying a child as gifted/talented. Louis and Lewis found that parents were correct 61 per cent of the time in identifying their child as gifted, with the remaining 39 per cent correct in that their children were advanced but did not meet the criteria for giftedness. Parent's reports are often dismissed as biased or as evidence of a pushy parent, but in actual fact most parents think that their own child is gifted and it is more common for parents to underestimate their children than overestimate, especially when the parents are well-educated.

Peer Nominations and Self-report

One form of identification that is often overlooked is peer nominations. Children in the classroom are very good at nominating gifted and talented students, as they have the opportunity to observe who finishes work with ease, or who helps them out to complete their own work. Peer nominations can be especially useful in identifying students from disadvantaged, culturally different or minority backgrounds. One example of a peer nomination exercise takes the form of a game of make-believer. Children are asked to imagine that they are stranded on a desert island and must name the classmate who would be the best organizer (leader, persuader), best judge (settles arguments, fair), fixer (improves things), inventor (invents, discovers), entertainer, etc.

Self-reporting should be used with older children who are often more self-aware and know their capabilities. Teachers may be unaware of the interests, motivations or extracurricular activities of older students, and in some cases underachievement may mask the presentation of abilities.

SPECIALIZED PROVISION FOR GIFTED AND TALENTED STUDENTS

The idea of specialized provision for gifted and talented students can be very emotive and can raise arguments ranging from accusations of elitism to the dangers of "hot-housing" young minds.

Arguments that differentiated provision for gifted students is elitist are most often levelled in the context of academic subjects. Our society strives for equality and fairness, so it seems unreasonable to give extra attention to those who are already highly able in languages, sciences or the arts. However, such an argument is rarely made when a student excels at music or sport. In those cases the student is rarely expected to stand aside and wait for those less talented to catch up but encouraged with private lessons and extracurricular activities. Such thinking implies that some gifts and talents are more valuable or more deserving of nurturance than others, which itself it elitist.

Another common attitude towards provision for gifted and talented students is that due to their abilities and potential, they already have the right tools for future success. Time and money instead needs to be devoted to the children at the "other end of the spectrum", those with disabilities and disadvantage to allow them the same opportunity to succeed. There are two compelling (and related) arguments to rebut this viewpoint.

Firstly, as previously mentioned and contrary to the popular perception, the gifted and talented are not a homogeneous group of hard-working, well-adjusted and achieving students, nor can we talk about a dichotomy between those who are gifted and those who have disabilities or learning difficulties. Children who are gifted and talented may also have emotional problems, adjustment issues, intellectual disabilities or they may be underachieving due to boredom, frustration, low self-esteem or stress. It is neither useful nor fair to attempt to categorize assume that just because they are gifted some students will not need further encouragement or help.

All pupils are entitled to an education based on their needs.

Secondly, all pupils are entitled to an education that takes them beyond the minimum basic skills and stretches them to develop their abilities as best they can. If we do not expect a student who is a talented sportsman to play less than his best because his age peers are not so advanced, why should a student who is gifted/talented in mathematics be required to sit quietly and wait until the rest of the class is finished or to complete more of the same sums to fill the time? Boredom often turns to frustration and underachievement and disaffectation with the learning process. The education system has a responsibility to provide an *appropriate level of challenge for students of all abilities,* not just those who may be classified under the traditional bracket of "special needs". This is true, even in cases where the student's potential performance will outstrip the necessary requirements. In her book "Too Clever by Half—a fair deal for gifted children", Carrie Winstanley gives an excellent overview of the range of economic, moral and educational viewpoints proposing and opposing provision for gifted and talented children that are not covered here.

PROVISION FOR GIFTED/TALENTED CHILDREN WITHIN THE REGULAR CLASSROOM

Curriculum Differentiation

Curriculum differentiation refers to the provision of different learning activities for same-aged children who have different learning needs and preferences. In dealing with gifted and talented students it is especially important to consider the extras that can be provided above and beyond what others in the class are studying. However, Sawyer points out that any extension activities must have be academically rigorous and that entertainment should not be mistaken for educational value.

Enrichment

It is important that teachers are willing to be flexible within the whole curriculum when providing for gifted and talented pupils. Enrichment implies horizontal flexibility whilst extension implies vertical flexibility.

Enrichment is any type of learning, or activity, which is outside the core of learning which most pupils undertake. It is additional to the established curriculum. It is a supplement to, not a replacement for, the core of work being undertaken. In a well planned and interesting classroom it may already be available. It can broaden pupils' horizons and help them to look at different aspects of their work. It may well be interest led. Enrichment could involve groups of pupils working together; it may mean working in a different way from usual. It should enrich the core and widen it out.

Extension

Extension is allowing, or enabling students to move through the curriculum at a faster rate than normal. It can mean 'acceleration', or skipping sections to move further ahead. It can also mean 'compacting' the curriculum so that it is denser and more complex. It should give opportunities to work in depth, and to work at the student's individual rate.

This vertical and horizontal stretching allows teachers to use work from other key stages of the national curriculum and from other subject areas, other than those generally being worked on. Flexibility in the national curriculum is recommended for gifted and talented pupils. They may well be working with pupils from higher age groups in certain subject areas.

Extension and enrichment may take place within a mixed-ability class, where gifted children are given further or more challenging activities to tackle, or alternatively there may be organized "pull-out" classes, outside of the regular class timetable, where extended work is tackled at a faster pace. When extension and enrichment activities are provided in the classroom, they should be sufficiently different from the material being studied by others in the class. Assignments that are intended to be extended or enriched work should not simply be "more work" that is doled out to keep the gifted/talented student occupied while others finish the original assignment, nor should it be "harder work" that they are expected to finish. Both of these measures may be perceived as punishment and may lead them to reduce their effort and become unmotivated.

Where extension and enrichment are operated as "pull-out" programmes and able individuals are grouped to work together outside of the classroom it is important that the class teacher can integrate work that the group have covered and build upon it. Further, students who take part in such pull-out programmes should not be punished by being expected to also complete the work that they have missed in class on extension activities, as again this can lead to a reduction in motivation.

Acceleration

Acceleration of children into classes beyond their age-group is a very emotive subject among both educators and parents. At present the leading academics on gifted education in India endorse the use of acceleration in appropriate circumstances when provision of the child's needs can be adequately met.

The aims of acceleration are

– To avoid boredom, and resulting behavioural difficulties

- To promote the child's development of good study skills such as higher-order thinking skills
- To allow children to mix more successfully with others, by placing them with children who differ in age, but share more similar interests
- To capitalize on young children's interests and abilities.

Research consistently reports that acceleration meets all of these academic, social and emotional aims. Accelerants mostly adjust well socially and emotionally and they report preferring to be with the older children compared to their age peers. A number of studies have found that children who are accelerated display no difference in adjustment compared with equally gifted children who were not accelerated.

Competitions

While competitions may not be marketed exclusively as vehicles for gifted/talented students, quite often they provide an excellent avenue for such pupils to work and to shine. At first glance they may appear to be passive entities, making use of talent that is already developed rather than encouraging new growth. However, they can activate and strengthen feeling for a particular subject, provide enrichment in researching a topic beyond its coverage within the curriculum, and development skills in problem-solving, perseverance and experimentation. If the competitors can choose the basis or topic of their entry, it can also provide a sense of autonomy that is not always readily accessible in curriculum-based schoolwork.

There is some suggestion that competitions tend to appeal more to boys than to girls and to those who are naturally more competitive, confident, and ambitious by nature. That said, they also offer potential for others to develop confidence and ambition if they are given the appropriate support and encouragement.

Mentoring

Gifted, talented and more able pupils can appear way ahead of their chronological age in their ability area. This may lead to unfair expectations of their social and personal development. Mentoring is a strategy that can work effectively with any age pupil and can offer intellectual and emotional benefits. On a basic level, it could be just finding someone to spend time with the child, talk at length with them and obtain a clearer view of their ideas, abilities, views and feelings. The mentor could be another adult, a teacher or even an older child. On a more sophisticated level, the mentor may have an interest, or even be an expert in the pupil's area of ability. If relationships with peers are difficult or stressful, the existence of a mentor can be very beneficial for defusing fraught situations.

Acceleration, enrichment and extension can all be used to good effect with gifted/talented learners in normal classrooms, without the need to create pull-out programmes. The following suggestions and activities give examples of how different learning styles can be employed that give the student the chance to use broad range of talents and to develop new ones.

As gifted/talented children may be advanced thinkers and enjoy the challenge of new tasks, one of the key themes in these approaches should be independent learning. Try to avoid "telling" the student new information; instead encourage them to seek it for themselves. Try to move towards more investigative, resource-based and active forms of learning.

Where possible, try to allow them to choose the method or activity that they would like to do in order to learn, as this promotes a sense of autonomy and "ownership" of learning. However, do encourage them to try new activities in order to broaden the learning experience.

Ten Approaches to Differentiation

1. *Task:* Children, either as individuals or groups, are given different tasks based on prior attainment. Able children can be challenged by setting tasks that encourage them to think at higher levels through the inclusion of problem-solving, investigation and the use of higher-order thinking skills.
2. *Outcome:* Children work on the same task following a common stimulus, but the teacher has different expectations for each child based on previous experience. Learning how to explain something to someone else so that they can understand a concept or process can be very challenging. An able child could be asked to explain or teach something to someone else, or write to someone else, or write or design something for children of a different age group.
3. *Pace:* Children are given a common task but the time allocated for completion is based on prior skills. An able child might be expected to spend less time completing the core task than others and may then undertake some more challenging extension work. Many able children miss the chance to do extension tasks where they are available because they take too long completing the core task, through lack of interest and motivation. Where appropriate, some children should be allowed to skip activities (known as 'compacting') and move quickly to extension work.

4. *Support:* Children work on a common task, but some receive more or less support than others. An able child may need help in weak areas of their own such as recording, use of ICT (Information and Communication Technology), developing study skills or co-operative learning.
5. *Resources:* Children are set a common task, but are given different resources, which require more advanced reading or research skills. Able children can be encouraged to use a range of resources or alternative methods for presenting their work.
6. *Grouping:* Children have a common task to complete but are grouped in a way that ensures success for all. Able children can sometimes be grouped with peers of similar ability and expected to perform at a higher level.
7. *Information:* Children are set a common task but are given different information, or different amounts of information, which can support or stretch their thinking.
8. *Role:* Children undertake a common task but individuals are given different roles. An able child could be given the role of the main researcher, or organizer of the group's information and resources.
9. *Homework:* Children are set different homework whilst some pupils may need time to complete work started in class. More able children might be given more complex aspects of the topic to research in more depth, or to carry out a different task.
10. *Dialogue/Using Questions:* The teacher adapts the questions they pose and the responses they make to different children. Differentiation by dialogue has recently been stressed as a key area to consider in meeting the needs of highly able children.

PROVIDING CHALLENGE FOR GIFTED/TALENTED STUDENTS

There is no catch-all definition for what constitutes appropriate challenge in school; however schools have a moral obligation to ensure that a pupil is not wasting her time on activities that are ill-suited to her level of ability. All students have the right to expect that they will receive an education appropriate to their level of ability. In the case of gifted and talented children, this may mean curricular enrichment, extended lesson plans, or acceleration through course work. It is neither feasible nor practical to suggest that the need for challenge must be met in every single aspect of the curriculum to the detriment of other students, but pupils should not be allowed to grow bored and frustrated.

Challenge and motivation are practically inseparable - in order to respond to challenge the student must have the interest and motivation to engage with it. Extrinsic motivation (from outside sources) such as the promise of reward or threats is rarely enough to sustain interest and application to tasks over time. Instead the pupil must have internal motivation and undertake the task through interest. As far as possible an able child should be exposed to a wide range of activities in order to find those that excite them most, and will continue to hold their interest if they are to work alone beyond the rest of the class.

Once the type of activity has been decided upon, the level of difficulty should be pitched in order to stave off boredom but avoid extreme frustration. If tasks are too easy the pupil may become bored easily, leading to disengagement or disruptive behaviour. Alternatively, if they can constantly achieve perfect scores on their extension activities it may reinforce their belief that they must always produce perfect work – a belief that can be damaging as they progress through school and work becomes tougher. Challenge must include a risk of failure, and it is preferable that students should learn to cope with failure in support environments to avoid the distress brought about by failure late in their academic careers.

On the other hand it can be very demoralizing if tasks are too difficult and the pupil can see no way to attempt them, especially if they are used to handling their regular schoolwork with ease. Children will intuitively struggle to attain something just outside of their grasp and to improve, giving the example of children in a playground who never injure themselves attempting outrageous stunts – instead they grow bolder as they slowly build confidence by trying slightly more daring moves when they feel able. Extension activities should aim to provide challenge that is just outside the grasp of the student in order to stimulate them, without seriously denting their morale.

SOCIAL AND EMOTIONAL ISSUES IN THE DEVELOPMENT OF GIFTED CHILDREN

At times there can be the perception that children who have been identified as gifted or talented are blessed with special qualities and advantages that will help them to succeed and make life easier for them. However, there is growing recognition that being gifted can bring with it challenges for social and emotional development, and those who are gifted are just as much in need of support as their peers in dealing with emotions, self-perception, behaviour and in looking to the future. That said, the idea of the gifted individual as a "mad genius" still prevalent in lay understanding is both unfair and inaccurate, and can lead to reluctance from parents to classify their children as gifted or talented. There is ongoing debate over whether gifted children have more or fewer emotional problems than their peers with some researchers claiming that they are better adjusted and others portraying them as emotionally fragile. As outlined the first sections of this chapter, gifted and talented children are not a homogeneous, easily-classifiable group. Therefore, we cannot infer that all gifted children will develop emotionally in the same way. While the following paragraphs outline the need for consideration of the emotional well-being of gifted and talented children, the behaviours discussed should not be considered *necessary* for giftedness.

The high intelligence, ability for self-analysis, perfectionism and creativity possessed by many highly gifted youth may lead them to evaluate themselves critically. The superior thinking strategies of gifted/talented children, including the ability to hypothesise and to consider multiple scenarios may mean that they are more likely to reflect on themselves and to understand and articulate the many facets of their behaviour and motives. Highly gifted and creative students will feel different; they will experience self-judgement, self-doubt, self-criticism and sometimes even self-loathing. They may also be more concerned than their peers with their purpose in life and in the world, and may display signs of extreme sensitivity and emotional intensity.

Self-concept, Self-esteem, and Identity

Problems and challenges associated with being gifted may begin early. From birth children who are gifted are often active babies who require less sleep, respond intensely to their environment and may physically exhaust parents with their demands for stimulation.

Once schooling begins, gifted children who find themselves grouped with same-age peers may find themselves in situations that meet neither their intellectual nor their social needs. This can lead to feelings of frustration and isolation and can lead to the development of poor social skills if they do not have opportunity to mix with others of similar interests and cognitive ability.

Academic self-esteem is often high in gifted (especially young) children; however social self-concepts are often poor. Some studies have shown that while children are pleased with the effects that being gifted had on their schoolwork, they disliked the connotations that it carried for them in their social lives, especially as they felt that non-gifted peers and teachers held negative views of them. Relating to this is the concept of labelling, and the discomfort it can pose to children who have been identified as gifted or talented in some domain. While the terms gifted/talented are often perceived by others as positive, they can be a source of discomfort for older students whose main desire is to "fit in" with their peers and who thus dislike being marked as different. Further, some adults find the terms distasteful as they go against the idea that "all people are created equal". They may even find the term threatening when it is applied to someone younger than them. One way to avoid the problems of labelling is to refer to the students' behaviour as gifted, rather than applying the term to the student herself. Thus, giftedness is not a quality that is bestowed on the individual but a behaviour (or set of behaviours) that can be displayed and developed.

Overexcitability and Extreme Sensitivity

Many highly intellectual or creatively talented students might experience emotion much more intensely than their peers, and display behaviours that are quite alien to their classmates, teachers and parents. Some of this emotionality can stem from their advanced capacity to wonder and hypothesize about scenarios. The ability to think about certain situations and follow them to conclusion can lead such children to be concerned about issues of social and moral justice, or environmental problems such as global warming. They may also have greater capacities for sympathy and empathy than other children their age. Although the word "overexcitability" has connotations that imply distress or even psychosis, in the context of theories of emotional development it was originally intended to denote abundant mental energy which provides "positive potential for further growth".

Family Relationships

Educators in the field generally agree that positive family relationships play a large part in shaping the development of the gifted child, and that the support of parents is crucial to the realization of full-potential. However, parenting a gifted or talented child may be stressful, and can strain both the parent-child relationship, and sibling bonds. While it is not universally true that problems will arise, raising a gifted/ talented child may present parents with unique challenges or unfamiliar situations that they did not have to tackle when rearing other children in the family. A lot of parents fear that they will have neither the emotional or intellectual coping skills to raise and support a "different" child. This feeling of inadequacy can affect the interactions within the family. Further, parents worry that their gifted child will grow up to be "socially maladjusted". Contrary to common belief however, some studies have shown that parents of academically talented students are not always guilty of being "pushy" and pressuring them to achieve. Although many parents in a longitudinal study programme defined academic success in terms of concepts outside the individual a large proportion also attributed success to internal factors such as happiness, attaining personal goals, trying one's best and being inquisitive.

A diagnosis of giftedness or talent may disrupt sibling relationships. There is some evidence that the siblings of gifted individuals feel greater jealousy and competition, and may be less well-adjusted than the siblings of non-gifted children. Gifted children may receive more attention from their parents than their siblings do, most likely because they are more demanding and require more stimulation, and this too is likely to cause competition and envy. However, it appears that difficulties among siblings are most intense soon after the label of "gifted/talented" has been applied; within five years the negative effects were negligible.

MANAGING STRESS IN GIFTED AND TALENTED CHILDREN

Stress can be defined as a biological reaction to circumstances where an individual perceives a discrepancy between a situation or event and their ability to cope with that event. Everyone experiences stress, and the extent to which we suffer is related to factors such as personality and temperament. Stress in gifted children can arise from a desire for perfectionism, feelings of being "different" from their peers, or worries that they cannot maintain the standard of work that is expected from them. Younger gifted children may find the classroom stressful if classmates constantly rely on them for help and support rather than asking the teacher. Often, young children would rather ask a classmate who they perceive to be "clever", instead of admitting to a teacher that they don't know an answer. While in small measures this may benefit the self-esteem of the gifted/talented child, if it happens regularly it can cause stress due to worry about falling behind with their own work, being caught talking when they shouldn't be, or being constantly distracted by others. Busy teachers may be happy to let more able pupils help their classmates, but often forget to convey the fact that they *know* they are helping and that the gifted child is not misbehaving, or neglecting their own work.

While challenge is necessary to extend and enrich the school curriculum for gifted and talented children, it is important to ensure that the challenge is not too difficult, or too far out of the reach of the child. Anyone if set near-impossible targets will find the situation stressful and it is wrong to assume that a child will relish tough challenges simply because they are gifted/talented. Extension activities should be graded in difficulty in order that the child does not move from the classwork they can complete with ease to a task that they struggle with, as this can be frightening and damaging to self-esteem.

Older gifted children may experience stress as they come to the senior years of the school cycle and the standard of work becomes more difficult. Suddenly the student who has always achieved straight A's with no problems at all may no longer be receiving such high grades, and they need reassurance that they are not "losing their giftedness". If this problem does not arise during the final years at school it often occurs in the early years at university, where it is no longer possible to maintain a 100 per cent record on assignments and examinations. Such a revelation can be quite damaging to the esteem of the gifted student, and again they need reassurance and preparation for this situation before they leave school. Also, students need to be reinforced with the idea that failure provides feedback and is an important part of the learning process. Gifted students may be particularly reluctant to adopt this view, especially if they have an unblemished academic record, so it is necessary to highlight the process of learning, rather than allowing them to continually focus on the outcome.

As end-of-year and school-leaving exams loom gifted students may experience intense stress as they struggle to live up to the high goals that they have set, to maintain their standard of work and "prove themselves". This problem can be exacerbated by teachers and classmates who dismiss them as "having nothing to worry about". Being gifted/talented does not alleviate exam pressures and may in fact intensify it, and these students need a trusted adult to whom they can express their fears and not have these fears dismissed as groundless. Further, hard-earned results deserve due praise and should not be dismissed with comments such as "we wouldn't have expected anything less from a gifted pupil like you". It is easy to forget the amount of care and attention that a student might have put in to their work, if they frequently turn in work of a high standard that appears effortless. Such comments are not only unfair to the student, but also explicitly state the weight of expectation that the student may already feel to perform well at all times in all subjects.

CAREER PLANNING AND SUPPORT FOR GIFTED/ TALENTED CHILDREN

Gifted students need help in relating their personalities, interests and abilities to specific career alternatives, and in understanding the personal requirements, training, lifestyles, advantages and disadvantages of different careers. Gifted and talented students often display multipotentiality, or the ability to succeed in a wide range of possible careers or fields of study. The gifted/ talented student with a diverse range of interests may be faced with a bewildering array of opportunities and may have real difficulty in deciding which career path they would like to follow. Common career aptitude tests may not be helpful, as often such students perform to a very high level on a number of (or all) subscales, leaving them unable to narrow down their choices. Highly talented students may profess that they could imagine themselves being equally happy studying modern history, engineering, philosophy or medicine, so how could they possibly choose? Equally unhelpful are career counsellors or parents who tell students "Well, with your brains you can do anything". Provision of work experiences, and mentors from industry and universities can provide students with a much clearer insight into possible careers and future study than hours poring over confusing university prospectuses.

UNDERACHIEVEMENT

The gifted or talented child who is underachieving represents both society's greatest loss and its greatest potential resource. Such children have the potential for high achievement, and yet are not reaching the levels of attainment that would be expected for individuals of their ability. This lack of attainment often leads in turn to frustration and annoyance in teachers, parents and within the child themselves. With appropriate interventions however, it is possible to reverse the pattern of underachievement and modify the pupil's cognitions and attitudes about work.

Underachievement is defined as a discrepancy between the child's school performance and some index of his or her actual ability, such as intelligence, achievement or creativity scores, or observational data. Although numerous different versions of this definition appear in the literature on underachievement, the key part to all of them is the discrepancy between actual and potential performance.

While such discrepancies are often easily picked up on in examinations, intelligence and attainment tests, some children may not perform well on any of these measures due to poor test-taking habits, and so the only way that they may be identified as gifted is through observation in classroom and home situations. For example teachers may note class behaviours, comments or vocabulary which hints that the child has more intellectual, creative or artistic potential than they are currently exhibiting in school. However, this requires teachers to be open-minded about the ways in which giftedness or talent can manifest itself – indeed, they must be open to the idea that a child who has previously been labelled as "average" or "below average" could have the potential to shine. Children who are highly creative may occasionally considered to be no more than average because their personalities and thinking styles are at odds with the traditional classroom. A lot of highly creative children express themselves through nonconformity, and this concern for thinking and acting differently from others compromized their ability to achieve and work to their full potential within the classroom.

Due to the frustration that teachers and parents may feel towards an underachieving gifted child, it is sometimes easy to label them as "lazy", or "wasteful of their talents". However, the roots of underachievement run much deeper than this, usually in socio-emotional problems that may in turn underlie certain negative behaviours. The characteristics of underachievement can be divided into primary, secondary and tertiary characteristics.

Primary Characteristics: Low Self-esteem

The characteristic that is most frequently and consistently found among underachieving children is that of low self-esteem. Often these students do not believe that they are capable of achieving the expectations of their family, teachers and friends and of themselves. In a sense, the problems of low self-esteem arise from the pressure to "be gifted". Related to this issue is a sense of personal control over the tasks in their lives. Pupils with low self-esteem may attribute failure to a lack of ability (rather than a failure to study adequately or appropriately), and success to good luck. Thus, they will take responsibility for their own failure but not their success.

Secondary Characteristics: Avoidance Behaviour

Low self-esteem often leads to unproductive behaviours based on the avoidance of work or study. This avoidance actually has a self-protective function – if the pupil has not studied then they can attribute failure to this, rather than having to question their own ability. If they study they may feel that they risk confirming their possible short-comings if they subsequently do not do well. In such scenarios pupils may also assert that they find the curriculum work "boring" or "pointless", as they feel that this provides further vindication for not studying.

Perfectionism and the expectation of low grades – although they appear to be opposites – both act as defence mechanisms for the underachieving child with low self-esteem. If the underachiever expects low grades, then she has lowered the possible gap between attainment and failure, meaning that she has at least achieved her (albeit low) goals. On the other hand, a perfectionist will strive for the unattainable, thus providing herself with the "get-out clause" that she sets higher standards for herself than others and so failure is not due to her own incompetence.

Avoidance behaviours are most common in secondary school students, although not by any means unknown in younger cohorts. Typically, those displaying poor grades and avoidance behaviours in the early to middle secondary school years had excellent school reports earlier on. Such reports include comments such as "impossible to improve!" or "wonderful student. Set for big things". It seems that the student's excellent performance and such high praise from teachers often led to perfectionistic tendencies. Later, when the school curriculum became more challenging, so as to no longer permit constant perfect performance these students became demoralized and avoidant of study. Onset of these behaviours may be as late as college or university for some students, especially those who consider themselves to be happy and interested at school without finding any assignments or study particularly difficult. Such cases highlight the need for all school work to be tailored to provide an appropriate level of *challenge* for every student.

Tertiary Characteristics

Because underachieving children avoid effort and achievement to protect their precarious self-esteem, tertiary characteristics arise which support the pattern of underachievement. These most frequently manifest themselves as poor study skills and concentration and/or poor discipline at home and school, but may also appear as peer acceptance problems. It is often these behaviours that provide the "tip-of-the-iceberg" indication that avoidance behaviours are masking low self-esteem. Also in this category are skill deficiencies. Gifted achievers and underachievers performed equally on tasks that required global or holistic processing, but where precision was needed in tasks with detailed computation, underachievers performed less well. If the gifted child finds writing difficult, they may prefer to focus on the verbal aspects of a task.

Gifted individuals may process information more quickly and at a more advanced level than others in the class and as a result will need challenging and enriching extension activities. If extra assignments are given that are simply "more" or "harder" types of the same work, the pupil may begin to view this "busywork" as punishment for finishing quickly and slow their rate of completion accordingly. However, as their mind still remains active they may occupy themselves with daydreaming, trouble-making or even reading other more exciting material. Over time these behaviours may acts as reinforcers that prevent the child from completing even the regular assigned class work.

Competitive classrooms where marks awarded are announced, or where a teacher expresses surprise at a student's high or low grades can have serious effects on gifted/talented children. Even students who are highly motivated and achieving may find that exaggerated emphasis on external rewards and punishments may detract from the inherent enjoyment that they get from learning. Those who underachieve may not have a clear picture of their competencies in certain areas, and receiving continuous feedback from teachers that they are not meeting expected standards may lead them to believe that they are actually below-average, or it may set in motion some of the avoidance or defensive behaviours outlined above. Finally, gifted children may be especially sensitive to an unrewarding curriculum because of their advanced facilities for analysing and criticizing material, or for the creative ways in which they think about subjects.

Gifted underachievers can often be seen to perform at a very high standard in extra-curricular activities where they have the opportunity to choose the type and level of the pursuit they are engaged in. Where possible this should be applied to the classroom by letting the gifted/talented learner choose the type of extension activity they would like to do thereby giving them the chance to exercise some autonomy over the curriculum.

EFFECTS OF CULTURE ON GIFTEDNESS AND TALENT

It is important to guard against the stereotype that gifted children from minority cultures will suffer due to deficient backgrounds and home lives. However, it is important to recognize that gifted students from such backgrounds suffer educationally because they are not identified as gifted/talented. This inequality is unacceptable as giftedness is assumed to occur with equal frequency in all cultures Minority cultural membership may also be a disadvantage when it is coupled with poverty, isolation or limited language exposure. It is further suggested that children from minority backgrounds may not show "traditional" signs of giftedness, as different values and skills are prized in different cultures, and so teachers may not be attuned to signs of giftedness beyond the norm.

Contrary to popular conceptions, socio-economic status has very little impact on individual children's academic achievement: factors such as parental encouragement of learning are much more important. Further, even when children are hampered by their family life, many show great resilience and with the help of some other significant adult in their lives as a mentor they can achieve highly.

Gifted/talented children who live in rural areas may be disadvantaged for a number of reasons, both in respect of developing their talents and with regard to identification and provision. Living in rural areas my mean children have less exposure to a range of social contacts from whom to learn; a smaller range of experiences to promote their development; fewer opportunities to come together with intellectual peers; and resources such as libraries, IT, and school support may receive less funding than in metropolitan areas.

SUGGESTIONS FOR CHALLENGING EXTENSION AND ENRICHMENT ACTIVITIES

1. *Resource-based learning*: You provide some resources and directions to follow so that pupils can find their own sources of information. You will need clear directions and parameters as to the areas in which they are researching. Allow for pupils to follow interesting tangents of their own.
2. *Supported self study*: This again involves pupils finding out for themselves, but usually supported by a study guide written by the teacher, which frames their investigation by areas of study, methods of presentation, time limits and so on. Pupils can work individually, in pairs, or in groups. Clear targets are set. End of unit assessment methods and areas are also known.
3. *Role-play:* This is not just 'play-acting' and should be introduced with care. It should involve careful research of the area to be presented, and of the parts the different 'role' or personnel play within it. A good role-play presentation would show a clear understanding of the key issues being researched, so these must be selected carefully either by the teacher, or in negotiation with the pupils involved. Participants should attempt to pull out the essence of the subject matter for presentation in this matter.
4. *Debating*: A formal debate situation can be set up so that pupils are deliberately researching one side of an argument for presentation to the group with the intent of influencing 'voters'. Again it makes for clarification of the key points around an issue, and also ensures careful listening, noting points to use later, making informed judgements, ensuring the facts are correct, waiting to make a point. Debaters will have to understand the whole picture to make an effective argument.

5. *Oral presentations*: Once more this requires a clear understanding of the area for presentation, and an ability to find and present the salient points. It also requires considered use of language forms, and vocabulary, and recognition of 'audience'.
6. *Poster making*: This is often seen as a method for the less able to present the point of view, and indeed can be used as such, but it can also be seen again as finding the most powerful arguments, and the most important points around an issue, and being aware of audience, so that the poster can be effective.
7. *Video making*: This task requires a number of skills and can be a challenge to the more able pupils to make an effective video concerning a topic they are working on. It will probably be a useful group task, with pupils designated to particular roles in the production team.
8. *Interviews*: This is an interesting process for pupils to decide which questions they wish to ask about a particular issue (a task in itself), and then to interview members of the public for facts and opinions. If a large number of interviews are done, then mathematical work can be done with the statistics generated, and it can be seen how statistics can be manipulated to prove a point.
9. *Creative writing*: Based upon the topic being addressed. Using pupils' imagination to create poems, plays, stories which illustrate the key points being dealt with. Again good background research and understanding will be needed to support such work.
10. *Art work and cartoons*: Another form of self-expression concerning the work being addressed in other subject areas. This will articulate what to the student are the most important points, and the

sequencing component of cartoon work is an interesting element.

11. *Book, film, newspaper reviews*: A useful way of gathering opinions and angles on the topic being addressed is to review books written about it, films produced about it, and newspaper articles written at the time. Poetry and stories written on the subject can be analysed for deeper content. Analysis of content of books, newspapers etc requires skills in selecting relevant information and opinions.
12. *Writing newspaper articles*: An interesting way of presenting the facts, whilst putting an individual opinion on them. Requires pupils to know the facts, and know what they think about them, and then to be able to present these things to someone else using ICT packages such as 'Front Page', 'PowerPoint', 'Publisher', 'Word'.
13. *Using statistics:* This can be an exercise in collecting and developing their own statistics, or analysing statistics already available to assess what they show; for example, perhaps about public understanding of a particular disability, or experience of sexual harassment; or opinions on women's role in society.
14. *Producing flow diagrams:* To represent a series of events (could be used in science, geography, history, story making and so on). This ensures a logical view of the 'flow' of events and clarity regarding key points which occur.
15. *Carrying out surveys: including questionnaires*: Surveys of local issues will be of interest and will involved detailed observation, counting, interviewing, producing graphs and statistics, and interpreting the information gathered.

16. *Organizing and running events:* Such as exhibitions, mini-enterprise and so on, any of which again involve detailed fact finding, assessment of key issues, good management of self and others, and of resources.
17. *Fieldwork*: Doing real fieldwork out in society.
18. *Problem solving*:Using facts and opinions gathered identify a 'need' or problem, analyse it, plan solutions, try them out if possible, evaluate.
19. *Pupil self-assessment*: Build in opportunities and methods for pupils to be involved in their own assessment. This can range from simple techniques such as self-marking of right and wrong answers, through groups analysing other groups' posters, role-plays and so on, to negotiating the value of a piece of work with the teacher. This, obviously, needs to be built into the setting of tasks with the pupils at the start of the work.
20. *Experiential learning*: Pupils put themselves in the position of the groups they are investigating, for example experiencing being treated as disabled.
21. *Using ICT*: Gifted and talented pupils often work more independently than others when making use of computers to research in greater depth. They should be encouraged to do this through opportunities both in school and at home where they may have better facilities to enhance the quality of their work.

SELECTED READINGS

Ainscow, M. (2005) *From Special Education to Effective Schools for All,* Keynote presentation at the Inclusive and Supportive Education Congress 2005, University of Strathclyde, Glasgow.

Alur, M. (2002) *Introduction,* in Hegarty, S & Alur M (eds) (2002) Education and Children with Special Needs: from Segregation to Inclusion, New Delhi: Sage Publications.

Amanda M. Vanderheyden; Joseph C Witt, Gale Naquin (2003). "Development And Validation Of A Process For Screening Referrals To Special Education". *School Psychology Review* (Research and Read Books, Journals, Articles at Questia Online Library) 32.

Balagopalan, S. & Subrahmanian, R. (2003) *Dalit and Adivasi Children in Schools: Some Preliminary Research Themes and Findings,* in IDS Bulletin, 34 (1), 2003, Falmer: Institute of Development Studies.

Bhambani, M. (2003) *Societal Responses to Women with Disabilities in India,* in Hans, A & Patri, A (eds) (2003) *Women, Disability and Identity,* New Delhi: Sage Publications.

Bhan, S. (2006) *Arm Them with Land,* in India Today International, May 2006, p.18

Blanchett, W. J. (2009). A retrospective examination of urban education: From "brown" to the resegregation of African Americans in special education—it is time to "go for broke". *Urban Education,* 44(4), 370-388.

Booth, T., Nes, K., & Stromstad, M. (2003) *Developing inclusive teacher education: Drawing the book together,* in Booth, T., Nes, K., & Stromstad, M. (eds) (2003) Developing Inclusive Teacher Education, London: Routlege Falmer.

Bowe, Frank (2004). *Making Inclusion Work.* Upper Saddle River, N.J: Prentice Hall.

Clough, P., & Corbett, J. (2000), *Theories of Inclusive Education*, London: Paul Chapman Publishing, Sage.

Cortiella, C. (2009). *The State of Learning Disabilities.* New York, NY: National Center for Learning Disabilities.

DFID (2000) *Disability, Poverty and Development*, London: Department for International Development.

Ellis, Edwin (2002). "Watering Up the Curriculum for Adolescents with Learning Disabilities, Part I: Goals of the Knowledge Dimension". *WETA.* Retrieved 2010-04-21.

Frederickson, N. & Cline, T. (2002) *Special Educational Needs, Inclusion and Diversity: a textbook*, Buckingham: Open University Press.

Freeman, J. (2001) Out-of-school educational provision for the gifted and talented around the world. A report for the DfES. http://www.joanfreeman.com/mainpages/freepapers.htm

GOI (2000) *India: Education For All Year 2000 Assessment*, Ministry of Human Resource Development, New Delhi: Government of India and NIEPA.

Hans, A. & Patri, A. (eds) (2003) *Women, Disability and Identity*, New Delhi: Sage Publications.

Heller, K.A. Mönks, F.J. Sternberg R. abd Subotnik R. (Eds.) (2000) *International Handbook of Research and Development of Giftedness and Talent.* Oxford: Pergamon Press.

Jangira, N. K. & Ahuja, A. (1994) *Teacher development initiative (TDI) to meet special needs in the classroom*, in Making it happen: Examples of good practice in Special Needs Education and Community-based Programmes, Paris: UNESCO, pp 43-53

Karen Zittleman; Sadker, David Miller (2006). *Teachers, Schools and Society: A Brief Introduction to Education with Bind-in Online Learning Center Card with free Student Reader CD-ROM.* McGraw-Hill Humanities/Social Sciences/Languages.

Ladson-Billings, Gloria (1994). *The dreamkeepers: successful teachers of African American children.* San Francisco: Jossey-Bass Publishers.

MHRD (1992). *National Policy on Education.* Ministry of Human Resource Development, New Delhi.

Miles, S. (2002) *Schools for All: Including disabled children in education*, practice guidelines, London: SCUK.

Mukhopadhyay, S. & Mani, M. N. G. (2002) *Education of Children with Special Needs*, in Govinda, R. (2002) (ed) India Education Report, NIEPA, New Delhi: Oxford University Press (pp. 96-108).

Nola Purdie & Louise Ellis (2005). "A Review of the Empirical Evidence Identifying Effective Interventions and Teaching Practices for Students with Learning Difficulties in Year 4, 5 and 6". ACEReSearch.

Otterman, Sharon (19 June 2010). "A Struggle to Educate the Severely Disabled". *The New York Times.*

Peters, S. (2004) *Inclusive Education: An EFA Strategy for All Children,* Washington DC: World Bank.

Priscilla Pardini (2002). "The History of Special Education". *Rethinking Schools* 16 (3).

Simpson, Richard L.; Sonja R. de Boer (2009). *Successful inclusion for students with autism: creating a complete, effective ASD inclusion program.* San Francisco: Jossey-Bass.

Singal, N. (2005) *Mapping the field of inclusive education: a review of the Indian literature,* International Journal of Inclusive Education, 9 (4), October-December 2005, pp. 331-350.

Tejeda-Delgado, M. (2009). Teacher efficacy, tolerance, gender, and years of experience and special education referrals. International *Journal of Special Education,* 24(1), 112-119.

Thomas, P. (2005) *Mainstreaming Disability in Development: India Country Report,* London: Disability Knowledge and Research.

Turnbull, Ron (2002). *Exceptional Lives: Special Education in Today's Schools* (3rd ed.) Merrill Prentice Hall. New Jersey.

UNESCO (1996). *Resource Teacher Education Resource Pack: Special Needs in the Classroom.* UNESCO, Paris.

Wilmshurst, L., & Brue, A. W. (2010). *The complete guide to special education* (2nd ed.). San Francisco: Jossey-Bass.

INDEX

38. Indian National Congress **(New)** 450/-
39. Indian Polity **(Revised Edition)** 295/-
40. New Comparative Government **(Revised Edition)** 295/-

Advanced Study in the History of Modern India

41. (Volume-1: 1707-1813) 225/-
42. (Volume-2: 1813-1920) 325/-
43. (Volume-3: 1920-1947) 175/-
44. Handbook of Nutrition & Dietetics 250/-
45. Development of Education in India 195/-
46. A Text Book of Environmental Studies 195/-
47. Teaching of History 175/-
48. Administrative Thinkers 195/-
49. Research Methodology 175/-
50. Curriculum Development 195/-
51. Teaching of Science 175/-
52. Teaching of Mathematics 175/-
53. Principles of Educational & Vocational Guidance 195/-
54. Child Psychology 175/-
55. Abnormal Psychology 175/-
56. Indian Education in Emerging Society 195/-
57. Human Resource Management 175/-
58. Higher Education and Global Challenges 175/-
59. Teaching of Geography 175/-
60. Teaching of Social Studies 175/-
61. Teaching of English 175/-
62. Education for All The Indian Saga 175/-
63. Value Education in Global Perspective 195/-
64. Teacher Training 175/-
65. Public Administration 175/-
66. Public Relations & Integrated Communications 195/-
67. Educational Psychology 175/-
68. Introduction to Educational Technology 175/-
69. Textbook of Food and Nutrition 175/-